"Fitness and Health, for the people!"
Straight, NO chaser

"FITNESS AND HEALTH,
FOR THE PEOPLE!"
STRAIGHT, NO CHASER

―――――――――――――――――

#DariusWrightthenaturalhealer

To order additional copies of this book, contact:
Xlibris
1-888-795-4274
www.Xlibris.com
Orders@Xlibris.com
794564

CONTENTS

FOREWORD

Fitness and Health, for the People! Straight, No Chaser

In health/fitness/wellness, Americans are being fooled. They are being tricked. They are being bamboozled! Most Americans today want to believe anything false that gives them an easy way out, an excuse to do all the wrong things! This is a book to empower the people. This is information that benefits the people, because so much of what is in existence today is designed to relieve us of our money, our health/fitness/wellness, and our very lives. The information here will give people the opportunity to make informed decisions about their health/lives and that of their loved ones. Medical science has made so much progress today that there's barely a healthy human left—in America that is.

The first thing you *all* need to know is your body's ability to heal is greater than anyone has chosen to tell you! You *all* have the ability to attain the greatest health and lives. You just have to have the knowledge, the pride, and the commitment to make it happen and it will. Your body is a reflection of the person you are and the life you are living! Don't let anyone deceive you into thinking you're supposed to be sick, and that sickness in your lives is inevitable.

Pharmaceutical companies are the drug cartels of today, doctors the drug dealers of today, the public, the exploited consumers of today! These are the integral parts of this equation of life, or should we say death, in American society. We must learn to think outside of the box. It's time to stop wasting time with illogical talk, and unhealthy messengers. Now you can have the power to dictate your own health and life. You've just got to have the knowledge, the pride, and the commitment to make it happen! You have to become educated consumers. Just like in every business, the less you know, the more they make. The less you care, the more they make. The more you believe in the lies they create to promote their prospective products or regimens, the more they make. It's *all* about business, and the medical/pharmaceutical businesses profit from sick people. Do you really believe that they truly have an interest in your health, or is it your unhealthiness that promotes their businesses?

I have personally gained the knowledge of life from suffering, through the experimentation of life itself, and from being on the brink of death for much of my life. Yes, I've been on the brink of death several times in my life, and have lived for decades a living hell. Today I've been blessed with the knowledge of life. Don't think that because I have attained maximum health I have great genetics or I'm just magically healthy at fifty-nine years of age. Don't believe that this knowledge came by miracle. It was gained from decades of suffering, at great physical and mental cost.

There was a time when I was just as limited in my knowledge, and probably more sickly than the average person of today, and that's saying something. I believed in everything you believe in reference to health, and that's whatever the doctors and pharmaceutical companies want us to believe. Those beliefs are why Americans are the least healthy in the world.

This is why I have written this book, *Fitness and Health, for the People! Straight, No Chaser.* This short book can give you, and yours, the basic knowledge of life and wellness. I have researched and discerned from literature, through numerous observations and through decades of experience, numbers of unhealthy and healthy people and found what is logical and what is not. Furthermore, through using myself as a "crash dummy" for over forty years, I've made observations of the totality of society, and I have understood these realities. I cannot be fooled by so-called science or dictated to by business—big business, pharmaceutical companies, and the Western medicinal industry. I and those whom I've learned from observed and realized these realities of natural healing, and now enjoy the maximum health found in this knowledge. In this short book, we can discover the fountain of youth, because it does exist. You too can receive the benefits and knowledge of life if you open your minds!

#DariusWrightthenaturalhealer here, promoter of health, researcher of realistic preventive health measures, natural health consultant/researcher, certified holistic practitioner, nationally certified fitness trainer, and former athlete.

In the very near future, the type of "health for profit" practiced in American society will be looked upon negatively for its barbarity and its illogical nature. No matter that the entire country is on chemical medications, no matter that children are epidemically obese and are getting diseases once reserved for adults. Most act and believe that this is normal. No matter that the whole of society maintains pitiful, nutrient-deplete lives, existing on chemical medicines and other unnatural therapies, which only serve to enrich the lives of those who promote them! Americans want to live in a fantasy world and are always looking for unrealistic, quick cures regardless of the long-term consequences. Many have been deceived into believing there are miracle cures, but look around, those things just don't work.

The people look at doctors and drug companies as the saviors of society when in reality they are contributing to the downfall of American society as far as physical and mental well-being are concerned, or should I just say the lives of the majority? They want to have the entire society drugged up and ready for the next medication, the next procedure, with no concern whatsoever for actual good health.

The public wants to be able to eat food that have little or no nutritional value. They want to drink drinks that are poison and of no value. They want to smoke cigarettes, drink alcohol, take chemicals for relief (whether legal or illegal), and then think that by not exerting the body with exercise, or some form of activity, that this recipe of unhealthiness somehow will result in good health. It doesn't help that the government, in essence, is in promotion of these ways. Whatever the charlatans of the medical/pharmaceutical business promote, the government backs with military arms!

Good health doesn't happen by magic. It won't happen from putting chemicals in our bodies or having unnatural surgeries performed. It takes a concerted effort through positive living habits.

Most Americans think being sick is the natural progression of life, and being fat, old-looking, dependent on drugs for health, and dependent on caretakers is natural and normal. Americans are the sickest people in the civilized world today. The medical industry tells them that they are genetically predisposed to all of the maladies of which they suffer, or that things just happen. The truth is, Americans are sick because of the atrocious way in which they live. There is never a thought that perhaps the companies promoting these sciences and products don't really have our lives as their main interest. They don't see that the industry needs them to be sick, unaware of the facts, and debilitated for maximum profit. Most Americans seem anxious to be on medicine or in cold, unhealthy doctor's offices, and even worse, these hospitals are only dens of unhealthiness. It seems as though these corporations, and doctors have stripped the very thought of physical health from the minds of the people!

Too many people are satisfied with being sick, and when you talk to someone that's unhealthy, they usually get very insulted when you try to offer knowledge, but if a sickly doctor or a commercial tells them of medicines and all of the negative side effects and gives them information, they are more than willing to listen. If something makes logical sense, or someone speaks knowledge that is of actual benefit, the public has no interest in that. Just like PT Barnum said, "There's a sucker born every minute." I say, "Thank goodness for the medical and pharmaceutical industry that Americans don't care enough about themselves or their loved ones to actually do something that makes logical sense in relation to their lives."

I have been a fitness/health consultant for over thirty-five years, but only in the last twenty-five years have I been enlightened about true health, natural health. I have written this short book because I am no different than any of you. I have grown up the way the majority of Americans live today, and that's totally unhealthy. I believed in—and was made to believe by my parents and the Establishment—about all the misconceptions that most of us believe in these days. I've tried everything out there, and one day I realized that none of that crap worked.

If you spoke to me of the natural or any other way of living except for the lifestyle lived by Americans as a whole, I thought you were a weird fool, a nut even. With only improper living and eating habits, my body and mind were totally in a state of imbalance, the result of not supplying the body with the necessary nutrients. Eventually, I ended up an alcoholic, cocaine-addicted, suicidal depressed mess, and the little food I did eat was mostly of food that were of little benefit. You know, greasy, deep-fried, heavy meats, no vegetables, no raw food, only highly cooked, overcooked, highly salted, heavily starched, processed, microwaved, genetically altered food, food that only destroy. You know, the SAD diet, the Standard American Diet—the diet most Americans are dying from!

The old adage that "you are what you eat" is not just a saying; it's the truth. If you eat dead or dying food, food stripped of life-giving qualities, you're depriving yourself of precious life, and you are promoting your own death. Scientists, doctors, pharmaceutical companies, and those who wish to profit from your unhealthiness always make the public think that optimum health is only attainable through great knowledge of science. This is a lie. We must learn the truth, and it's more simplistic than you could ever have imagined! It is science, but not science filled with jargon and fancy theories, just the simplistic and logical truth.

Why Would You Want Anything Other Than the Healthiest Life?

I have written this short book to make you think logically. What we say here will cure no one. It is only the first step toward empowerment. There is definitely a "fountain of youth," and it was never lost. It was and is lost in the minds of a so-called technologically advanced society. A society that thinks that they are now superior to the natural environment that created them, of which we come from! In the Amazon rainforests alone, but also all over the world, there are hundreds of thousands of cures, nutrients, and life-giving products/substances that most have no knowledge even exist! This is the knowledge we must attain, to maximize our health/lives, and no longer depend on those who depend on us to be sick, keep them rich, while we know nothing but suffering and costs.

Look around, statistically Americans are the unhealthiest people in the civilized world. We are the most obese and have the highest incidence of preventable diseases. You know: high cholesterol, high blood pressure, cardiovascular diseases, diabetes, cancers of all types, gastrointestinal disorders, skin disorders, oral disorders, depression/the mental disorders, to include the addictions, and all of the common ailments, that can be explained away, with a diagnosis of malnutrition in the great majority of cases. By reading this book, at least you can say that you have the

1

foundation for knowing right from wrong when it comes to your health. We become empowered in our knowledge of ourselves and the bounty of substances available and the amount of activities that we can engage in to live long, caretaker- and medicine-free lives.

After this short book, it is your responsibility to gain as much knowledge of all things that are in the interest of your health. Remember, as a rule of thumb, *if something sounds too good to be true, it is!* Find and read books that make logical sense, that focus on natural healing, nature, and those things manifested by the earth. Listen to those who seem to understand the realities of nature's bounty, not those who want to cash in on your unhealthiness, but fail to help you to become healthy. When someone talks to you about health, look at them closely: Do they follow what they say, or are they just talking you to death, trying to get your money, or impress you with jargon? Are they themselves healthy, or do they look old and fat and need help and knowledge just like you? The one thing we don't need when trying to get healthy is a bunch of talk. Don't waste time with that. Action and implementation is what we need to get the job done and our lives in balance!

Just the very same as in all businesses—and medicine is a business—the less you know, the more you can be taken advantage of, and the more knowledgeable you are, the less the likelihood of you being exploited. This is only plain fact. In business or in life in general, people only get done to them what they allow, or what they don't understand. Isn't it always the most unintelligent or the uninformed that can be manipulated and cheated? This is the plight of most Americans today. Yes, people are telling them what they want to hear, but what they are being told only compromises their health and lives. Of course they tell us things like, "We can take fat off in so many days," or "Our machine is the key to fitness, and you'll be fat free," or "This pill is your key to health," and always, "Surgery will be the key to your cure." Sounds good, but the truth is, none of these are the key to life, and you've seen all the failures, by either yourself or others. In the back of your mind, you know that junk doesn't work, but you still hope and pray. There is no need to hope though, because everything you need is available in abundance throughout the earth, and the rest is up to you.

My short book will tell you the cold hard truth: There are no miracles, except for the miracle that is the "Mother Earth." Only she holds the key to our and all of life's existence. Man has known these things for thousands of years, but they never knew why. Now scientists know why, and they extract components of plants and other substances from the pure Mother Earth when making chemical medicines. What they don't realize is that as they extract, they destroy the life energy, which makes the chemical beneficial in the first place. In doing so, the substance has become unnatural, harmful, and poisonous to the body. This can only cause imbalance; therefore you need another drug to counteract those effects, and so on and so on. Anyway, there's not much profit in selling plants, and there are no side effects, so there is no market for another drug to counteract the other.

This is plain logic. Do you really believe that all things necessary for us to thrive are not provided by the earth? Do you believe that man-made poison is the cure, which leads to maximum health? We consider ourselves to be creatures of God. Do we believe that God would leave his children so vulnerable? Everything for us to have quality life, cosmetic beauty, and good health is right here, all around us. We just have to learn about the numerous substances provided for our lives. This is the most valuable education that you can receive. Stop thinking that man holds the key to your life. You have seen the hordes of people sustained by chemicals and the knife, I don't think that's something that most people strive for: looking, being sick, incapacitated, and old!

I want this to be a wake-up call. Men, you don't need Viagra. You need exercise and nutritious food. Women, you don't need hormone replacement or bariatric surgery. You've got to live the way nature intended! Even if you don't care about yourself, remember that our children usually do and emulate what we do. If we show them wrong things, this will become part of their psyche. The foolish ways of living we have taught them will only continue a cycle of sickness, disease, and death.

Let's change it. It's time we wake up and stop eating and drinking like mindless barbarians. This is the twenty-first century. Are we not more intelligent than this? Learn to do for self. The only true help is self-help, and always do for self! By reading this short but informative book, you will find it to be your key into the door of realizing that the "fountain of youth" really does exist!

Good Health to You All!

#DariusWrightthenaturalhealer, holistic practitioner, nationally certified fitness trainer, natural health consultant, and researcher
www.teslalonglife.com

Before any healing or wellness/fitness can be attained, we must first stop doing the things that got us sickly, overweight/obese, or unfit in the first place! It's time to start doing the right things so we can enjoy the lives we have been blessed with. We all can attain the greatest health and life simplistically, but it has to come naturally. The great problem in society today is that people are trying to get healthy once they get sick. Instead, they must stay healthy to prevent from ever getting sick in the first place. Preventive health and wellness is how we attain and maintain high-quality life.

We don't need fad diets, expensive doctors, numerous available toxic chemicals, and so many tricks and gimmicks designed to take our money while doing nothing for our health and lives. If we use the substances that provide the pure energy provided by the earth found in all the natural food and substances, then we're energizing our lives and maximizing life. The more we utilize what is pure and natural, rather than what most Americans use, the more balanced all our body systems will function. When our lives are only inundated with man-made products and unnatural substances, health and life are always compromised. When you see the numerous amounts of unhealthy people in American society, that is the result of unhealthy lives, from unhealthy living in the great majority of cases. Earthly life can only thrive from the life-giving energy of the earth and the sun, found in the plants, animals, and other naturally occurring substances.

When we live according to the rules of nature, using only what nature has provided for our lives, then this is the way we can create positive, disease-free, doctor-free, and medicine-free life. When we use unnatural food, products, and substances, all we are doing is putting poison into the bloodstream and cells. This is the root of unhealthiness, and this is what creates sickness, diseases, poor-quality health, and early death, as far as the preventable diseases.

It's time we learned to live life as it was intended, not the way people in America are living today, killing ourselves first by eating, drinking poisonous substances, not exercising, and then looking for a cure from this poison through other poison (chemical medicines) or the knife (surgeries). Just look around: Almost everyone is fat, overweight, or obese, sick-looking, prematurely aged, with the look of death, and/or the lowest possible energy.

People are on every type of medicine, on every type of drugs (legal and illegal), a cigarette smoker, an alcohol drinker, and then have little choice but to eat/drink the least nutritious food and substances. We're inundated with genetically modified food, processed, microwaved, chemically created so-called food, since that's mainly what's available. To top it all off, with the follower mentality of the society and the massive addictions of the internet, fewer and fewer people are staying active, which is a death sentence for them. Everything that most are involved in these days causes major stress upon their bodies and will even destroy parts of the body like the eyes and brain, in internet addictions. These people then wonder why they are sick, unhealthy, old-looking, and have numerous issues. It's because what they are doing is the perfect recipe for sickness, diseases, poor-quality health, and early death.

Remember these important facts: The body cannot regenerate itself when it's full of inflammation, mucous, parasites, toxic chemicals, heavy metals, excessive hormones, dead-animal flesh, cooked mucous-forming dairy products, refined sugars, genetically modified and processed food, which only help to decimate our health and lives.

We have to understand that there are no miracle chemical cures, special diets, cocktails, or machines to get us healthy and fit. Whether we want to believe it or not, the only way to achieve long life and good health is by the old-fashioned way. We have to earn it by following the prescribed "recipe for wellness" or some semblance of that! We have to do *all* the right natural things that promote health and life.

There is no one thing that we can do to attain wellness. It's a systematic process of living in the right ways. Today there are many charlatans touting this natural thing, and that natural thing as the miracle cure, beyond even chemical medicines. There is *no* one thing—it's the combination of numerous natural ways we must engage in and do every single day for the rest of our lives, or most of those days anyway. There is no cure in that sense. What it is we must begin to live right lives, if we want a right life.

If we take humans from the beginning of life, breastfeed them, feed them only food of the earth in their natural form, greatly minimize the eating of meats, maximize the eating of life-giving plant food, and eliminate the food most Americans eat, stay active, and keep stress out of our lives, then we will have people who can attain the best possible health and lives. You will have a body that functions in the way nature intended, one that generates life—and that means eliminating negativity, sickness, and diseases.

There Is a Recipe for Wellness

When we eat the food of the earth that were provided for our nutrition and lives, utilizing the beneficial substances from the earth (which are numerous) such as the common natural food, herbs, superfood, sea life, and other naturally occurring substances, we can achieve optimum health, or should I say the only way that will result in the highest-quality health.

We must learn about absorbing the life-giving energy of the natural environment. Educate ourselves about absorbing nutrients/life transdermally (through the skin), through baths, massage, acupuncture and use of oils, essential oils, the mineral salts, and other naturally occurring substances, which all contain the various and numerous nutrients of life. Every manner of nourishing the inner and outer body must be learned and known.

Then we must learn about movement, physical work, and/or some form of exercise or perpetual physical activity. Those are the only true but simplistic ways of achieving optimum health. Eating right and exercising are the essential building blocks toward wellness, but not the only ways toward wellness and health. There is much more to learn than just mere eating right and exercising.

You can follow all the fads in the world, you can listen to every unknowledgeable charlatan, you can let doctors cut you to pieces with surgeries, you can take pills till your heads fall off, you can buy all the synthetic commercial powders, but the only person you're fooling and hurting is yourself. Those things just don't work, and they can't work because the substances contained in most of them don't come from nature or have been greatly compromised or refined so they don't contain the necessary life energy to support the cells. They contain *no* life-giving energy to support and sustain our lives, or are simply gimmicks to take your money, or keep you sickly for exploitation by the medical pharmaceutical business. Those various tricks and gimmicks makes them money until your untimely death, but only after great suffering, sickness, diseases, and, of course, profits for the medical/pharmaceutical business.

There are many societies around the world with people who have enjoyed the greatest health and lives for thousands of years now. The one constant is always living a simplistic and natural existence is the key to health and longevity. In America, we have sacrificed good health for modern ways and technology. Just look around; it's not working.

Think about it this way. Look at those who have been at the very brink of death from living totally unhealthy lives, eating all the wrong food/drinks, or engaging in risky lives, drinking liquor, doing drugs legal and illegal, and so many other things that devastated their lives. Or even those who've been catastrophically injured and were at the doorway of death. Those who've tried every diet, every machine, who lived so foolishly, and of course nothing ever worked, or helped and they continued in a downward spiral of depression, then almost death. If they survive all of that, many times they are looking to live a life opposite of what put them at death's door.

After years and maybe decades of suffering, then coming to the brink of death, maybe several or numerous times, being constantly sick, and/or never feeling well, then finally, after all the suffering, all the pain, they've seen the light. They then begin to live in the way nature intended and do those things that promote their lives and not destroy it. They've learned from being so close to the brink of death that if they don't do what is right, right now, they won't have a life to be worried about. They decide and realize that they can live extended, high-quality lives if they stop doing the wrong things. And they are absolutely right. People are having so many problems today because so few are doing the right things! Once they start doing the right things, in every way, they magically get better, or at least it seems that way. It's not magic; it's nature!

After being at death's door or suffering a living death for basically their whole lives, or even just a portion of life, these people now want to live life to the fullest potential. Life is short, and health wise, unpleasant when we live the way the average American lives. Those near-death experiences and the numerous mistakes made just living life and suffering from just systemic poor health are the best teachers. The knowledge I have attained today in wellness is because I have been so close to death several times in my almost six decades. I had to gain this knowledge, or I would already be dead.

I lived for years a living death. The terrible life I once lived and those near-death experiences totally opened up my mind and made me realize the realities. In my decades of experience, I've tried all the available tricks, gimmicks, and medicines, and I believed in all the same lies that most do today. They just recycle themselves through the decades, waiting for the next group of suckers. I once totally trusted and believed in Western medicine because I knew of nothing else. They've been tricking folks for a long time, and in the end many of the tricksters always die early from unhealthiness, but many, or most times rich, to leave legacies for their family. Yet whatever they promote, in a few years they decide that it's no longer the right way, that they were wrong, or that it had a negative effect on health, and sorry so many of you had to suffer and die. But never fear, the legal industry will pick up the cases, and then they can make their trillions and billions from the lives of the people again, or should I say after the suffering and/or death of the people? When we live according to the rules of nature, we never have to worry about anything but doing the right things, and that will increase our odds of a good life, one hundred times or so. In this way, we don't allow others to play Russian roulette with our lives and profit from our unhealthiness, while our lives go the opposite of health!

Education/Knowledge
Is the Key

Just look at the people promoting chemical meds, chemically made products, unnatural, synthetic products, and the sciences associated with them. Usually sick-looking old men, weak and unhealthy young men, or overweight women who look as if they could use some good food, exercise, and some sun, or just plain average, unhealthy people who have no business speaking on health and wellness because they don't have that. Why does the whole society believe in these people when they don't exude life energy themselves? They are just as sick as everybody else! They just have the gift of gab, which obviously the majority fall for, but they never receive positive results. Doctors and others who work in Western medicine of today are not healers but promoters of chemical concoctions and unnatural ways that could never lead to health. They are mainly in it for the great profits, while the majority continue great suffering.

There are no quick fixes. Optimum health can only occur in the natural order, simplistically and through absorbing life energy, nutrients and other life factors. This generates life within our cells and bloodstream. This promotes life throughout the body. This is an environment that is conducive to good health.

There are no quick fixes. We have to do all the right things! This is a phrase we will repeat over and over again. *There are no quick fixes!* Chemical medicines can work in a totally healthy body, but the problem is that almost every one of the people on medications in America are those who have the lowest immune systems and health possible. Medications devastate those chronically unhealthy people and only lead to a cycle of more and more chemicals, while the body becomes more and more imbalanced/sick. Furthermore they believe that the medicines are a miracle cure since their doctors lead them to believe so, and so they continue to live the worst possible lives while putting new poison into the blood to counteract the old poison. How can they heal when they don't stop doing the things that made them sick in the first place? It's impossible is the answer.

And just as there are no miracle chemical cures, there are no miracle natural cures! Many things in nature are a part of the cure, but not the whole cure. The cure is prevention, and living in the right way in the first place, so when we utilize the numerous natural substances/remedies on a regular basis or in an emergency, they work. Like we say though, in a strong body, even the chemical meds can work. Those things can work because our bodies are already strong, already viable, and exist in a healing mode constantly. When we live in this natural way that *all* the healthy people on earth live, then we can enjoy maximum health and life. So if we contract something beyond the scope of natural healing, our strong systems will allow chemical meds to work as designed. The more simplistic and natural the life, free of medicines we live, the more beneficial to our lives. Poisons are not what the body and cells want and need, but in emergency situations, you have to do what you have to do.

"The **doctor** of the future will no longer treat the human frame with drugs, but rather will **cure** and **prevent** disease with **nutrition**."

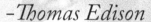

–*Thomas Edison*

We must educate ourselves because much of the information available is simply propaganda to promote Western medicine, profits, and not the lives of the people. Education will be our key to not being exploited by the secretive elites or charlatans of the medical and pharmaceutical industries. Those people are only concerned with profit, but unconcerned with our health and lives. Please don't delude yourselves. This is not to say there aren't some good doctors out there that actually want to do some good, but it's rare, and they don't have the right knowledge of healing in most cases, just pharmaceutically based science and methods. Really if there were many who actually know healing, would America be in such an epidemic of unhealthiness?

Does it make sense that doctors, who are some of the highest paid in society, or the pharmaceutical companies, who are some of the richest companies in the world, really have your health at heart? If we are healthy, then there will be no great need for either of these industries, and they won't have those very large bank accounts, million-dollar homes, and those expensive lifestyles. If we are educated to the substances that the earth has provided for our sustenance and lives, live opposite of the unhealthy majority, then our lives and deaths will be in our own hands, not the hands of those who profit from our unhealthiness.

Think of one instance when man-made concoctions really cured, or do they just continue a cycle of illness with more and more medicines. Yet the FDA, CDC, and such are designed to protect the people, really protect and promote the medical pharmaceutical businesses. But let me make this statement one more time: In a totally healthy body, their chemical medications can work as designed, but how many totally healthy people are there in American society? This is the conundrum with Western medicine. If people lived healthy lifestyles, instead of unhealthy lifestyles, Western medicine would actually work, but would be far less necessary. Today they have numerous medications, with more side effects than the disease they were designed to cure.

So let us not be fooled. I am for technology in the control of diseases not of a preventable nature such as in impoverished nations or even the modern world. Diseases such as malaria, smallpox, measles, Ebola, the plague, and leprosy, which are an epidemic in poor societies because of their lack of sanitation, nutritious food, and the most necessary resources. Then the diseases of the modern world, the preventable diseases in their advanced/death stages like cancers, heart disease, diabetes, AIDS, multiple sclerosis, and the newly created antibiotic and medicine-resistant diseases such as MRSA or Staph infections, flesh-eating bacteria, and so on. Some of these are newly created diseases or have been made to manifest in the so-called modern world from the overprescribing of antibiotics and other chemical meds.

Of course we need Western medicine for catastrophic injuries and those things outside the realm of natural healing. We must have technology to combat these killers, but too much technology is the reason for the multitude of powerful drug-resistant, genetically altered diseases we have today. Doctors liberally and casually prescribing antibiotics and chemical medications for every little thing have caused many strains of diseases to mutate. When we allow the body to rid itself of disease, through proper natural living, diseases lack an atmosphere conducive to breeding and multiplying. In other words, diseases have no basis to form in an alkaline, fertile, or mineral-rich bloodstream. Diseases can't and don't manifest in a fertile/alkaline, mineral-rich bloodstream. A toxic or acidic bloodstream or toxic internal environment is the perfect breeding ground for diseases. The great majority of Americans have the most toxic bloodstreams. We must live in a manner that eliminates a toxic bloodstreams or toxic environments. In this way we eliminate the onset of sickness and diseases. This is why so many Americans have pain and diseases of inflammation. Their bodies lack the necessary building blocks of life, the necessary minerals. With a body full of minerals and the other life factors, we are living in a preventive manner, maximizing health and life.

This is not to say that no one will ever get sick. The human body is a sponge, and not concrete or plastic. Germs and pathogens will enter the body. The key is to live in a manner that the body can rid itself of such things before they manifest, or minimize their effects once they have entered our systems. That means living a totally natural lifestyle. There is no other possibility. This is why in the modern world, to catch diseases like measles, mumps and such, is actually the true immunization. It's illogical to believe that by extracting various strains of diseases, mixed with chemical poison, that that will manifest immune function. The reality is, such things decimate the body and the cells, while causing sometimes, or most times, lifelong disruptions and imbalances. Combine that poison with genetically modified food, the most toxic food like products, poisonous personal and home and outside products with a totally toxic environment. It's only a recipe for sickness, diseases, and early death.

Of course the pharmaceutical-companies-bought-and-paid-for science recommends the usage of their products, with paid-for science to back up the claims! I know about the damages of vaccines from a personal perspective, and although as a child I was forced by full restraint to take those shots, the reality is there was something inside me that knew those things were no good. I suffered numerous childhood ailments now associated with vaccines, but back then they were just chalked up as normal childhood diseases and ailments that everyone got. I also had a diet comparable to these days, not the healthy diet of those times.

So not only was I vaccine poisoned, I was also totally nutritionally depleted. Of course no one from my past remembers things the way I do; they never do, but I remember all the sufferings vividly, so my memory can't really be debated on that. Today the numerous things I suffered from are what everybody has. The only difference back then, because we were so active playing and such, that few were overweight or fat. In fact, I was too skinny and undersized for many years. The food and products were nowhere nearly as toxic as the products of today.

What I suggest for any and all parents: Do your due diligence, but remember the information you are getting supporting vaccines is information bought and paid for by the companies that manufacture and sell them! You have to think logically. Do you really believe that the companies who profit in the billions from these products, and then more, and more billions from the numerous side effects, imbalances, and reciprocal diseases that stem from those things, care about your lives? What does history tell us about the government and big business?

Right eating, drinking, staying active, absorbing the energy provided by the natural environment, soaking in mineral-rich baths, using only natural substances for internal and external health are some of the keys to maximizing life. The use of only living, natural substances promotes a fertile environment internally and externally. All cellular growth and maturation comes from the products we put into and on our bodies, so we must learn to maximize the amounts of life-giving energy from substances of the earth (natural substances) that we use. Our cells only recognize those substances that come from what we come from—nature, the planet Earth! Natural substances are compatible with our DNA or cells. Really they are one and the same. Those substances that do not contain DNA or corrupted DNA are adverse to our lives. Most of the products in American society today fit that description, however.

Where We Can Find the True Medicine

Those natural plants and food from all over the earth and other naturally occurring substances are the true medicines provided for our lives. However, when man strips those plants and synthesizes them, or refines them, they destroy the life-giving abilities and render that plant into a synthetic, man-altered product/substance, which makes it no longer a life-giving substance. This becomes poison to living organisms, or unhealthy for the cells. Such things cause imbalance. Such substances lack the life energy to promote and sustain life. We need to get into our systems the whole plant or the whole organism as nature intended.

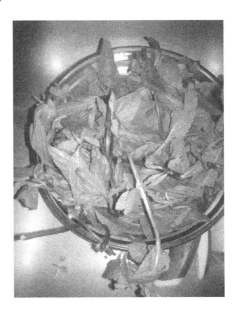

As adults we full well know that anything worthwhile, 99.9 percent of the time, takes consistent habits. Obviously, by the obesity rates and all-around unhealthiness that we have in America, people are not interested, or at the least not following these standard rules. Consistent not meaning intense, but meaning it takes a change in lifestyles, mentalities, and upbringings, instilling a discipline that will directly relate to improved health and quality of life. Which means you'll have to get up from the couch and move, get out in the natural environment, eat the proper food, drink mineral-rich waters, utilize substances from the earth that assist and allow the body to function as necessary to rid and/or protect from diseases to actually be healthy.

These aspects are very difficult for the average American to absorb, because we always want the easiest, fastest way to the ultimate body, or we want to magically achieve health and wellness. Such things are an impossibility without the most deadly or adverse side effects anyway! Also many Americans love cheap, crappy, low-quality, fatty, dead food, and we bring our children up on these poisonous substances, and that only manifests unhealthy life. No positive health and life can be achieved from such an existence. Those unhealthy, commercial substances contain *no* fuel, *no* life-giving energy for our lives, and it destroys our and our children's health and lives!

LIVING ON THE SAD DIET

Bad food—the food most Americans eat—are poison. They are dead, they contain no life, and they can promote *no* life or health. The Standard American Diet, or SAD, is devastating the lives of Americans. The numerous unhealthy and unnatural food in American society contains little or no nutrition to promote and sustain life. It doesn't contain living nutritional substances or the energy that nourishes the cells of the body. It doesn't contain the energy needed for the life of the cells. It is one of the main reasons why the body begins to die/deteriorate/degenerate, and just because death isn't instantaneous doesn't make them any less poisonous or deadly. Dead food is processed, overcooked, highly salted, highly sugared, chemically enhanced, microwaved, fast, junk, commercially promoted pseudo food. They may look like real food, but they are only representations of real food.

We are inundated with billions of dollars' worth of advertising, promoting junk/bad food, unhealthy products, as well as downright deceiving products that are promoted by the food industry, medical/pharmaceutical, and fitness industries (everyone mostly just wants your money). Yet we empty our pockets, thinking we can cheat evolution and nature. Man cannot upstage nature, no matter what you want to believe. The body will only accept those substances and ways that are natural and will only develop through natural living. You can get positive-looking cosmetic results from chemicals, but the look is unnatural; the side effects will always be unhealthy and, ultimately, deadly.

Our bodies don't accept/recognize the unnatural chemical or the synthetic, the genetically altered, the un-nutritious products altered/refined by man. They are incompatible with our DNA. Just because your mind tells you it's something good, or someone who profits from your unhealthiness tells you that those things are beneficial, you only have to look at that big belly and that sagging old-looking skin to know that the food or products you have been eating/using or the things you have been or haven't been doing for health and life are the reasons for your compromised health. Once again, the cells can only recognize and absorb those things that come from nature. If we want to have healthy lives, then we must embrace every aspect of nature. When the body has no life energy to absorb and no nutrients to promote growth, it's in a state of degeneration or dying since there is little to no life energy to energize and sustain the cells. In such a state, suffering and early death are imminent.

Why Eat Natural Food?

Real natural food of the earth are provided to promote our health and lives. Food are not for filling the stomach with whatever you like, but was provided as fuel for the cells to generate growth, and for the body to function in keeping a balance that results in high-quality life. Food that is unacceptable to the cells are the unnatural food or synthetic/pseudo food. Wrong/unhealthy food toxifies the blood. They create acidic environment conducive only to poor health and wellness. This is an atmosphere conducive to sickness and disease, created from living toxic life. Purification and proper nourishment of the body and its systems is the ideal we must search for, and this cannot be accomplished by inundating the body with unusable, unhealthy, toxic substances. We have to do *all*, or most of the right natural things for the rest of our days!

Americans are dying much earlier than we should be and living low-quality, chemical- and caretaker-dependent lives when it is unnecessary. Bad food or toxic substances, they say, are food, are not acceptable to our cells. If they were, they would be absorbed in the bloodstream, and the cells of the body would relish their existence, not store them as fat and waste material that constantly poisons the blood and cells. This storage of waste causes the body's systems to be imbalanced and unable to function as necessary. Food and substances that are unnatural disrupt the natural balance of our bodies. That in turn compromises immune function, making us susceptible to sickness, diseases, poor-quality health, and early death.

The Only Possible Way of Achieving Long Life/Health

The only way to achieve long life and health is by living in the way that all components of the earth are to live. We must have clean fresh air. There must be photosynthesis, meaning extracting vitamins and energy from the sun, and extracting the energy provided by the food and substances energized by the sun. We must have clean, mineral-rich water for hydration of the body, since the body mainly consists of saltwater, which is needed for the electrical conductivity of our cells and the proper mineral balance. We must mainly intake our energy sources (food) from life-giving substances such as fruits and vegetables, herbs, superfood, grains, legumes, and ocean life. We must learn to absorb the energy of the living environment by consistently engaging in outside physical and mental activities. Dead material such as excessive meats and other non-life-giving synthetic substances or non-living substances such as synthesized food, processed food, genetically modified food, and overcooked/burned food should be kept to a minimum or totally eliminated.

We must make ourselves understand that chemical medications, bad food/drinks, cigarettes, alcohol, illegal drugs, and the majority of the things and vices Americans engage in totally devastate the body. They contain absolutely *no life*. They're only poison! They are poison to our cells and body. That aspect may be difficult for some to fathom, but there are always alternatives in life, so if long life is desired, we must do what is necessary for good health and long life. If you want the best health and life, then let the poison go. There are millions upon millions of unhealthy people in America for you to realize the results of such a life.

Pride in Oneself Is Paramount to Wellness

You have to have an internal desire, a pride, so to speak. I don't believe that anyone actually wants to be overweight/fat, unhealthy, and out of shape, but many people are just plain chronically tired from the lack of life energy, and as they age, they lose their sense of pride and many abilities. Furthermore, we are inundated with products, advertising, and media that promote nothing but unhealthy things, and unhealthy mentalities constantly. I do believe though that most people do not understand that this unhealthy state of living is the reason for the onset of most diseases and ailments in American society. People think the many diseases Americans have come from genetics or by magic. They don't comprehend that the totally unhealthy lives they live are the reason they are sick and unhealthy. When we live according to the rules of nature, health and life are manifested.

When we live in an unhealthy manner, the results directly affect all systems of the body adversely. Conversely, good and healthy living directly correlate to a healthy mind and body, and so saying, all systems work cohesively against cell degeneration and disease. Cellular degeneration causes disease, the excessive destruction of health, and excessive aging. We *must* discipline ourselves in such a way that we can have both cosmetic external beauty and internal superior health. The results will speak for themselves.

When was the last time that you saw someone that lived a healthy, proper life, according to nature's standards, that didn't look well and full of life energy? You can always tell those who don't live according to the standards of nature—their bodies look like something that the life is being drained from, and so it has! Some of these people are underweight, but mostly overweight. Many are prematurely aging. They have less energy than what is normal. Their body's systems cannot function as necessary since they are filled with toxins and little that manifests life. This puts the body's internal systems in constant imbalance and stress, and since Americans are in a constant state of toxicity, this makes them ripe for every manner of sickness and diseases. In such an environment, does it seem likely that life can flourish? This is the most important question you must ask yourself.

I Personally Grew Up in a Very Unhealthy Lifestyle

As a child I existed on a diet high in bad fat/grease, sugars, salt, and chemicals. You know, like the way most people live today, however, I was always undersized and never heavy! I was frequently sick with every manner of ailment, inside and out. My own mother recently says to me that when I and my sister were children, we were rarely sick. That is the lie she has convinced herself of. The reality was far different. My skin was that of an iguana. I had horrendous acne as well as horrifying dermatitis and eczema. I also had a numerous cavities and oral problems. Eventually as a young adult, my devastated systems led me through a deadly bout of constant depression, alcoholism, and drug abuse. I now know that this poor diet was a main contributor toward this mental imbalance, but not the only one, and to many of my health problems.

My life now is virtually disease free. I have beaten suicidal depression, alcoholism, and drug addiction, and I believe I can be an inspiration for those who also live unhealthy and/or addicted lives. I have worked with many in the communities with substance abuse problems and the youth, trying to get them to avoid such problems, which is easier said than done. It's never too late to be healthy or learn about healthy living. It is known that the body can and does reverse adverse problems, the body can and will heal itself when giving the right opportunities at healing through nature. I am living proof!

The Pathway to Unhealthiness

This is what my diet consisted of as a child, teenager, and young adult: sodas and highly sugared drinks like Kool-Aid, burgers and fries, fried and starchy food, overcooked meats, nothing fresh, surely no fruits or vegetables, along with a constant/daily diet of candy and every junk food available. These were my food of choice as a young child, but I shouldn't have had that choice. My mother and father, though college educated and highly intelligent, had no inkling of proper diet and its correlation to good health, nor did anyone at those times (the 1960s and before). She and most others of that time were under—and are under—the impression today that disease is an inevitability of our lives, and that we are supposed to get sick. Also, since they totally believed in the effectiveness and knowledge of doctors, whatever those so-called doctors said was like *gold*. It's far worse today though. People are far more unhealthy today than in the sixties and seventies, where really people weren't unhealthy. In 2019, America is the least healthy developed nation and has an epidemic of every manner of negativity in health and wellness.

Doctors and the medical/pharmaceutical business tell you that if others in your family had an affliction a generation before, so shall you—the so-called genetic passing down of diseases. In my childhood family household, all of us suffered from stomachaches, headaches, stomach viruses, frequent colds, terrible coughs, and such on a regular basis. It's obvious to me today that those almost daily sicknesses were brought about by totally imbalanced systems from very poor diets. I know now those many sicknesses were the results of malnutrition from eating wrong food, food of no value to health and life. Foods that aren't even real food, they're nothing but junk. My mother said in reference to that frequent sickness, "Those things were inherited." I thought to myself, "From both sides of the family!" Mom and Dad had the same problems. We all did. I knew something was wrong when she said that, but what would I know?

Many Americans in society don't have the level of education my mother and father have. They know even less, if that's actually possible. Americans know really nothing when it comes to knowing about proper living habits and life. That's why everyone is so unhealthy, yet they actually believe they eat right and live right and are healthy. When I go out in public, so many exude the look of unhealthiness, but many are proud and could care less about making change! They have been deceived by propaganda, and those who profit from unhealthiness, to embrace their unhealthiness, regardless that it's an early death sentence. These many preventable diseases Americans suffer from aren't from genetics, but from abominable living.

Being Manipulated for Profits

Science never tells us that the continuation of unhealthy lifestyles and eating food that promote disease are the most likely candidates for the onset of obesity and preventable diseases. The truth is that unhealthy living is the reason, and it's only logical. No wonder people who eat and live undisciplined lives end up obese, contracting such maladies as diabetes, high blood pressure, heart disease, cancers of all types, gastrointestinal disorders, oral disorders, skin disorders, depression and the mental diseases, including addictions of every manner, and so much more. Now they are coming up with newly found ailments every day that could all be eliminated simply by right living.

Obesity is a form of malnutrition. Malnutrition (lack of nutrients in the bloodstream) is the recipe for the diseases that are manifested by obesity, the so-called preventable diseases that so many Americans have. We must end the cycle of ignorance and live in the way nature intended! And are we really so smart—our brother the gorilla (97 percent of human DNA, our close relative) exists mostly on plant matter, and I know of no human stronger and more healthy than the gorilla. Let's not forget about elephants, hippos, rhinos, cattle, and so on, who live only on plant matter and have strength hundred times that of humans! So who is that telling us to build up on animal proteins? The most unhealthy thing for a gorilla, or any of our animal brothers, is contact with their filthy eating cousin, humans! Like I have said before, I am not advocating for not eating high-quality meats, just mainly plant food and other natural substances that are far greater for health. Gorillas are true vegetarians; chimpanzees and humans are omnivores.

You've Got to Get up and Move

The next aspect after proper nutritional health is the physical movement, exercise, physical activity of some type. The main thing to always remember: Exercise is fine-tuning. You can't outexercise a bad diet. Exercising in gyms and such is also supplemental to the work we should be doing in the natural environment. It can't replace actual work, but it is better than doing nothing. However, gym work can specifically target and expand athletic training, whereas work is simply what the body needs to be able to function as necessary, and without adverse health. Without the proper nutrients in the body/cells, which is the fuel for our body/cells to function, the body cannot function as necessary, so exercise is of little value in a malnourished body.

This is why you see many people in the gym, yet they aren't achieving the necessary benefits or results. Although they are better off than those who do nothing, eventually they will fall into the abyss of sickness and disease of those who do nothing, or all the wrong things. Maintain a well-balanced diet, along with utilizing those natural substances other than the known food, provided by the earth, like the superfood, herbs, other naturally occurring substances, etc., and that will give you the ability to achieve the internal balance of life necessary to attain/maintain optimum health and optimum fitness. You can't attain one without the other, or the attainment of one without the other will only ultimately result in failure.

Lack of nutritional wellness, fitness, and necessary health are the main causes of obesity, heart disease, diabetes, hypertension, circulatory problems, cancers of all types, respiratory disorders, arthritis, and even the mental disorders and addictions. Why should we incur such scourges of the body, not to mention the financial burden, and the lack of cosmetique beauty, just because we don't want to eat, drink, sleep, and exercise regularly/properly? If we put as much effort into right living as we do alcohol drinking, cigarette smoking, overeating and eating wrong food, not to mention material endeavors, then we could put that effort into eating right and living healthy, don't you think? People strive to live life to about forty then they believe that, or it's almost over. Kids forty years old think they are old! Sixty is only half the human life cycle, so it is only their perception that they are old that is making them old.

Many end up saying, "To hell with exercise and eating right. You gotta die of something!" How foolish we are when we think there is no other road but the course we're already traveling. We must learn to change the course of negative life. Make your course one of good health and long life!

THE FOUNTAIN OF YOUTH REALLY DOES EXIST

Yes, there is a "fountain of youth." It was provided by nature millions of years ago, and man with all his technology has found nothing better, although they deceive the gullible public into believing such things. Just look at any hospital or doctor's office, or simply go out in public. So many people are living totally unhealthy lives. People think they can upstage nature, but no one seems to care that everyone is sick, unfit, and unhealthy. It's really impossible to upstage nature. The body readily accepts what it comes from—the earth. Therefore, it cherishes and relishes nutrients and ingredients from nature. It does not readily accept the man-made, the chemical, or the synthetic, and in most cases it rejects the substances, which then promotes bad health. Those substances not from nature are poison to our cells. They don't contain the living DNA, or life-giving energy of the sun, to promote and sustain our lives. They promote degeneration of life.

Just watch any pharmaceutical commercial, listen to all the allergic reactions they list. The so-called cures have more side effects than the diseases. I say don't even listen to the food commercials, since most food offered in the American market is highly inferior, genetically modified, and mainly toxic to life/health in the long run! That's why we must learn how to work with the earth and learn about the cornucopia of substances she has provided for our and all life. We must also educate ourselves about natural farming practices and use the vote to stop the poisoning of our food and environment. When we use what the earth has provided, we can achieve long life and good health! You can easily see the results in society of those who lives have been cursed with man-made food, products, and substances. The bad part is, they have been totally convinced that whatever is happening to their lives from all this poison is perfectly natural, or from family genetics and such.

In almost every other culture and society, there has been a resurgence of naturopathic medicine or natural healing and in most societies, a diverse natural diet is the acceptable norm. In many societies natural healing has been a part of their cultures for thousands of years. Look at the Indian people from India, and although many of them are now chemical doctors, the Ayurvedic natural medicine has been in existence for thousands of years there. The United States, in all their infinite wisdom, has not accepted nature's own health products as they once did in the past, instead choosing to profit from nutritionally stripped food and medicinal plants stripped of their living properties. Scientists have now broken down fruits and vegetables, and evidence of the nutritional diversity is now fact. We are now aware of the various vitamins, minerals, and other essential substances necessary for optimum health that food from the earth contain. In the past, they knew of the healing properties of natural substances, but didn't know how or why they worked. Today only the very few can comprehend the facts of natural healing.

However, Americans in the medical/pharmaceutical business choose to profit from and utilize chemical concoctions and other man-made products that they know or don't know in the long run will be detrimental to the body. Why should the companies care—without our ignorance of health, there can be no profit? It is our own responsibility to investigate what's best for our own bodies. No longer should we rely on others for our own life and or death! That's not saying that doctors and medicine don't have their place, but we have allowed too much invasion on our own health, to the detriment of society. "Heal thyself" is the motto! Doctors should be the last line of defense, not the first and only. No human should be on multiple chemical medications for a lifetime of suffering, but many are, and believe this is normal.

We must be more conscious of our own health, for all involved, and remember it's not all about you. I'm sure most of us have family, which is a major component in our mental and physical health. Also our children follow what we do. If we are obese and sickly, the odds are, so will our children. We must teach our children to live to achieve the greatest health and life, and not to promote their death through unhealthy and ignorant living. When we are healthy and fit, life is good for all concerned. A family that stays healthy and fit together can live long life together.

You Can Look and Feel As Good As Is Humanly Possible

First, let me say that everyone has a different makeup, yet we are all the same. Not only are no two fingerprints alike, but no two people are exactly alike! In saying this, many people in the medical, fitness, and health industry depend on charts and graphs for many things, such as body-fat ratios, fat-to-height ratios, to man-and-woman ratios. I say throw all this crap out. You cannot judge people by charts. Each individual and their specific needs must be addressed. We are basing our measuring sticks on the perfect human, of a certain race, and although there are some who fit these categories, the general public does not. So we go through life trying to look like movie/TV stars, body builders and athletes. That's not going to happen unless you're willing to put in the necessary work and we shouldn't be deceived into believing that it's possible otherwise. You can, however, look and feel as good as is possible, within the standards of our own genetics when we live in mainly or preferably a positive manner. The more things we do of a positive nature, the more positive the results we will receive. We all have the same abilities to achieve the greatest health and lives. Don't ever let charts and those with a lot of talking, fancy degrees and certificates, fancy videos and jargon dictate your lives.

We are talking here about natural health, normal long-lasting health. It must be a lifetime commitment. There are no set amount of weeks, like "We promise to get you healthy in twenty-eight days" or such advertising. You must decide whether you want to be a sick, out-of-shape shell of a human being, dependent on medicine just to exist, or do you want to live a thriving, enjoyable, long life. I've trained/consulted and have seen many senior citizens through the years. They are my motivation to continue to live a healthy life. I've frequently seen people in their seventies and eighties working out, looking good, and cheating the Grim Reaper out of a new member.

Theoretically, each day eating the right food, putting in the maximum amount of nutrients, putting time in the gym, or preferably the outside environment, is another day added to our life expectancy. I have no medical statistics to this fact, but I can see—and I and others I am currently observing—prove this beyond a shadow of a doubt. People who refuse to exercise and eat right are always the ones in the hospital, at the doctor's office, and at the pharmacy. They are always bent over, overweight or underweight, have lose or pale skin, and coughing, looking for the next medicine or the next surgery. Some of the seniors I used to see in the gym are vibrant and full of life, and it was very motivating. They haven't gotten there by doing the wrong things! In fact, it has been said that this generation will be outlived by the generation before them. Just think about it, there are more healthy people over the age of seventy than people in their forties! Well, it sure looks that way! You've got to keep it moving, and never, ever stop!

When I was a child, I thought forty was old. At fifty-nine, I'm looking down on the average twenty-five-year-old, and none of my friends seem to get the message, and the ones that don't are all unhealthy and old-looking. Let's suffice it to say that they look like grandfathers and grandmothers. I don't like to think about it, but many of the people I have known in life are already gone. All they did was smoke, drink alcohol and hardly any water, and eat fatty, fried, no-vegetable diet, or should I simply say the *sad* diet, and exercise was out of the question. Combine that with the massive stresses of such a life, and this is definitely the best recipe for poor health and slow or sudden death.

Since the beginning of the writing of this book, countless people that I have known in life—some celebrities, some I've known personally—have died, most of them from plain old unhealthiness. Regardless of the disease the chemical doctors named them, those early deaths could have easily been prevented with right living.

THINKING OUTSIDE THE BOX

So we must forget everything we have learned about health, eating, and fitness. We must relearn what a proper way of living is all about. We must learn to eat like humans are supposed to, understanding that food was provided by nature and these must be eaten as close to their natural state as possible to get the maximum benefit. As children, we were taught all the misconceptions that we now have in reference to health and wellness. We weren't taught about healthy diet because if we were, then there would be no great need for doctors and synthetic medicines. We must realize that medicine as it is now is about making money; it is very big business.

The longer you are unknowledgeable, sick, and unhealthy, the longer you will be an asset to the medical industry. I see no real evidence of doctors teaching patients about preventive health. All I see is them pumping chemical after chemical in already sick bodies. These infusions of chemicals never allow the body to come into balance since they contain *no* nutritional value or life energy for the cells. Eventually, the body becomes dependent on these chemical medicine, which only continue a cycle of imbalance, poisoning, and eventual disease resistance to drugs, as is evident today. Doctors have zero knowledge of preventive health. Their knowledge is based solely on pharmaceutical science, and that is science based and predicated on profits!

What most people in America don't realize is that Mother Nature has provided more than enough substances for us to minimize the use of man-made chemicals. I feel it is the duty of all personal health personnel to educate themselves and then the public on preventive health measures for long, meaningful life! And if they aren't educating you on a natural path, then they are obviously misinformed, not educated to the facts, or interested only in financial gains. In any case, it is your responsibility to realize what's logical. We are all part of a fantastic system: nature. Everything on the planet is relative; meaning, all systems are basically from the same basic origins and exist in unison with each other. We must eat the food, and absorb the energy of our natural environment of our own existence! All these different, unnatural things being promoted and forced upon the people, mostly with the approval of the people, are the reason why people's lives are cursed with so much sickness and disease. It's surely not by magic, geographical location, or any of that crap. It's by design of the companies who profit from such things and they make multibillions from all angles of the situation.

This is why we must eat properly and eat/drink only natural food/ substances. Eating food that contain pure life energy, such as fruits and vegetables, help the body to naturally burn fat, which helps to purify and strengthen the blood. Also, they are fibrous in nature, so they naturally bind fat and eliminate both fat and wastes, which most American bodies are inundated with. It is as simple as this: plant a watermelon seed and you get a plump juicy watermelon somewhere down the road. Plant a dead pig and all you get is decay.

The same thing happens in the body. Dead food (meats, processed food, GMOs, synthesized food, microwaved food, chemically enhanced food) are of little value to the body, are stored as toxins, decaying matter in the digestive tract, and tissues of the body. This toxic waste invades all systems of the body. They create mutations and clog the blood stream, causing stomachaches, headaches, irritability, and skin and oral disorders, and then those minor illnesses evolve to maladies such as cancer and high blood cholesterol, or the many viruses, bacteria, and infections that attack the body when our immune systems are so compromised. When you look at a grossly overweight body or simply an overweight body, you are looking at toxic waste, and this is why we must cleanse the body of these toxic materials. Toxic food and substances must be eliminated from our lives if we want to attain the best lives. Toxicity of the blood, which compromises immune functions, is one of the main reasons for the onset of negativity in health.

When you look at that protruding belly, that is actually your stomach storing garbage, toxins, waste, and fat. In essence, you become a toxic waste site. Instead of fighting disease, the body must work on ridding itself of these toxins! With the way most Americans live, it is impossible for the body to catch up as they continually flood the body with more and more toxins of all types, and never give the body the pure fuel needed to promote health and life. Life can't flourish in such an environment; life is drained in such an environment.

Intake of as much fiber and water, plus exercise, is essential in elimination of these wastes, and in doing so, we create an atmosphere conducive to growth and life. We must also learn the other substances that the earth has provided to assist our bodies in fortifying or strengthening health, and that work in the elimination of substances harmful to the body. Find good, logical information on natural healing and health. The bible of health for me has been *Prescription for Nutritional Healing* by Phyllis Balch. This is a necessary good starting reference material for all those seeking optimum health; however, look for any literature provided by reputable natural healers.

Once again, I won't advocate not eating meat; for some, this is out of the question. So therefore, I would recommend for those who must have meat (which is most of the general population) to reduce the intake, diversify the types of meats, and always try to ensure it's of the highest quality if you are financially able.

I always promote a 90/10 regimen, which means 90 percent living plant food, and the rest are some types of animal products, if wanted. Red meat is the most difficult to digest and is therefore the most adverse to the system. Pork and chicken are white meats and are more easily digested. Many people believe that pork is high in fat, but red meat seems to have a higher content. That fat, if not in excessive amounts, is beneficial to our lives. Either way, reduction in portions is essential. A senior citizen told me one day: "You can eat anything provided by the earth as long as it is in proportion, and moderation is the key."

To add more health to the diet and less dead matter, add plant food or fiber to the diet. Fiber, meaning the plant food, is one of the greatest sources of living energy that we can ingest and the main source for those animals we eat for sustenance.

Your fruits, vegetables, sea vegetables, beans, superfood, herbs, and your grains are what we are speaking about. Without these substances, the body cannot function properly, since the body would be rendered toxic and would be totally clogged. With no fiber in the diet, food will just decay in the digestive system, where toxins filter throughout the body, causing damage, excessive weight gain, and disease. Just as we must wash the outer body, we must more so do with the inner body. Without fiber, the body remains full of filth, causing major disruptions throughout the body. Fiber is soluble or insoluble and is cellulose in nature, although there are other types of fiber such as chitin from seashells, and marine fiber. They all perform the same essential tasks: providing life-giving energy/nutrients, combined with the binding of fat and cleansing of dead/toxic material from the body, which is essential for optimum health.

A Few Good Sources of Fiber and Bioavailable Nutrients

---

1. Fruits
2. Vegetables
3. Grains
4. Nuts
5. Marine phytoplankton, sea vegetables, marine algae, sea kelp, etc.
6. Psyllium fiber (high-fiber colon and digestive cleanser)
7. Legumes (beans)
8. Herbs

Probiotics and Digestive Enzymes for Health

Another crucial part of digesting food so that the body can more easily extract the necessary nutrients and remove the necessary waste is the digestive enzymes and probiotics. These substances are natural derivatives of yogurt culture and fruits like papaya and pineapple. These vegetable enzymes and friendly probiotic bacteria break down food so that they can be made ready to be utilized and then absorbed or eliminated by the body and cells. More importantly, they create an atmosphere that is conducive to good health, since they strengthen the immune system with good, beneficial bacteria and enzymes. Bad bacteria and other toxic organisms are prevented from colonizing the digestive tract and are replaced with those organisms that promote growth and good life/health. I will say to you that, although every part of natural health is of importance, this must be considered at the top of the list. I will not list all of the various types of beneficial enzymes and probiotics, it will be your responsibility to investigate and educate yourselves to all of the realities of life. However, you may begin your search with acidophilus, FOS, bifidus, kefir, etc., and other naturally fermented products.

With the extremely terrible and barely nutritious food of today that can barely be digested, if at all, the digestive enzymes and probiotics need to become your good friend.

Fat Burners

I don't recommend other dietary fat burners, such as ephedra, caffeine, or ma huang, because they are potentially dangerous and the utilization of these herbs has other purposes. We are in no need of such fat burners since the diverse diet that we should be living on will be the only fat burners we need. As we have said, life-giving food burn fat naturally! For balanced health and the generation of life energy, this will be a continuous commitment as the main portion of our lives. Just eat right, exercise regularly, and live according to the rules of nature. That's the ticket! There are *no* quick fixes, but it is simplistic. You're going to have to earn that good health and wellness the hard but beneficial way by doing *all* the right things!

You'd Better Learn About This

The life-giving benefits of mineral salt baths

One of the many ways I always utilize to strengthen my health and life while also detoxifying is my mineral-rich baths. Use any of the numerous beneficial mineral salts to detoxify, alkalize, and mineralize your body. When we soak in mineral-rich baths, our bodies absorb the nutrition from head to toe without the destruction of stomach acids and such. Soaking in mineral-rich baths promotes healing from the outside in and promotes external/internal health and beauty. If the skin is healthy and vibrant, then that is a reflection of the inner body! If the skin is pale, dry, sagging, bumpy, sick, and unhealthy-looking, then that, too, is a window into the inner body.

Some of the more common mineral salts are:

1. Dead Sea salt
2. Himalayan salt
3. Magnesium chloride flakes
4. Red alaea salt
5. Sodium bicarbonate
6. Epsom salts
7. Sea salt

It's natural, safe, and inexpensive; however, remember that Epsom salts are the weakest of the lot and easily dissipate.

People who eat a Western-style diet consisting of sugar, red meat, cheese, and other refined food have a high acid consumption, which mineral salt baths can neutralize. You can also detoxify your body from alcohol, caffeine, nicotine, and chemical medications.

Use only sodium bicarbonate with your bath to relieve pain from hemorrhoids, vaginal yeast infection, anal irritation, and other irritations in the genital or buttock area. Baking soda soothes irritated skin, relieves itching, and reduces that burning sensation. However, other mineral salts could cause great discomfort and burning, so you must keep that in mind.

Baking soda is an excellent substitute for commercial products used for bathing. It does not contain fragrances and chemicals, it is colorless and odorless, and it leaves no residues in the bathtub. It makes bathwater alkaline and leaves the skin feeling silky and clean. It's a very inexpensive way to get a nutrient-rich bath.

Some Other Types of Baths

1. Oxygen Detox Bath

Fill your tub with warm or hot water. Add two cups of hydrogen peroxide and one-fourth to one-half cup of boiled ginger juice from fresh ginger, or squeeze in the juices of some fresh lemons or limes. You can soak for thirty minutes or more. Oxygen detox helps in cleansing nasal congestion, alleviating body aches, and relieving allergies and skin irritation.

2. Clay Detox Bath

Add a half a cup of Dead Sea salt, Himalayan salt, red alaea salts, magnesium chloride crystals, or combination of any, in warm or moderately hot bath. Add essential oils. Mix a quarter cup of bentonite clay in a small amount of water in a glass jar. Use a plastic spoon, and with vigorous motion, dissolve the clumps, then add to the water. I suggest putting a bentonite mixture on as a clay mask on the face and other problem areas of the body. Let it dry completely. Get in the bath, then soak for about twenty minutes. Add nut oil like coconut, or olive oil, black castor oil, hemp oil, or whatever you desire. Now, you're learning about healing from the outside in.

Educate yourselves to other healing from the outside in, such as massage, reiki, acupuncture, and other natural modes of healing. You'll find that they are far more beneficial to your lives than anything unnatural.

A Change for the Better

We must now realize that the most important aspect of our lives is not our job, it's not our cars, not how big our house is . . . but our own personal health! Without our health, we are of no use/value to ourselves or good for our loved ones. We won't be here to enjoy them or to add to their lives!

My former lawyer worked himself to death for over forty years. Yes, he made millions of dollars, but guess what, he won't be enjoying any of it! He would not change his habits, implement an exercise program, proper sleeping habits, or proper diet. Looking at him, the results spoke for themselves—he looked like the living dead. What sense does it make to work oneself to death? Since the writing of this book, he has passed on! Such is the life of too many in American society today. It's especially devastating when you know beyond a shadow of a doubt that it didn't have to be that way. If he would have stopped, listened, and learned, he could have reversed that death march, but he wouldn't, so he didn't!

The purpose of life is living, not dying! So it has to be a lifetime commitment. Don't worry that you slipped one day (although the objective is not to slip); that just means you've got to work that much harder in the gym the next day or preferably in the natural environment, drink plenty of mineral-rich water, increase the amount of fiber, continue our usage of enzymes and probiotics, or drink one or a combination of the many available teas from herbs and roots, or juices from fruits and vegetables to cleanse out the crap. A natural intestinal cleanser to get the crap out is ok, and never stop, just keep on going, and keep on pushing. You're not going to be perfect, but knowing how to minimize the damage we may possibly do is imperative to our lives.

Don't set unrealistic goals, though; we're not trying to win a contest. All we want is usable life; life without the need for medicine, caretakers, and doctors. We want to be in control of our own destiny. Eventually, through consistency, you will evolve to not even desire the things you may desire today because healthy life changes most aspects of our lives to a more positive mentality. You could easily attain a mentality that craves good health and life while cursing unhealthiness.

Consistency Is the Key to Wellness

What counts is consistency. I am not one these new jacks who are into the tricks and gimmicks of fitness and wellness. I'm the biggest believer in doing things the old-fashioned way, the natural way. It will not, however, hurt to keep a daily diary of what you are eating for your own knowledge, and if you feel it necessary, keep record of your exercise regimen. As long as you're eating right, exercising, getting the proper sleep, keeping stress out of your lives, and taking some of the substances from nature that boost the bodies systems, you're way, way ahead of the game.

You will look younger than what others in America perceive your age to be, that's for sure. You will feel younger than a person your age is supposed to feel. It's all up to you. The more you put into living correctly, the more you'll get out of it, but remember that you are in no contest! Just keep doing the right things, keep it moving, keep it going, and the results will speak for themselves.

I do know for sure that once you start getting healthy after being unhealthy, there's no way you'll want to go back to being the way you were, in many cases. It's just like being an addict: once they're clean and see the benefits of clean living, who would want to go back to that dirty, unhealthy life? Yes, I know many drug addicts fail as well as food addicts and every manner of addict, but at the heart of it all is, did they care enough of life to make the change? Was the stress of their lives, too overwhelming for them to bear, one of the considerations? The same thing happens with the person that is addicted to wrong living, which when combined with those other dysfunctions and problems, decimate our lives.

If You Truly Care About Your Lives, Then Continue . . .

Let's ask ourselves some basic but hard questions.

1. Are you happy with what you see in the mirror?
2. Do you feel uncomfortable in public about your appearance?
3. Are you satisfied with being unhealthy and unfit?
4. Do you think that being unhealthy is just part of life?
5. What can you do to better yourself?
6. Do you have what it takes to keep yourself healthy?
7. Is there any part of your body that looks ok?
8. Would you be embarrassed to be seen in the nude?
9. If you were in shape and healthy, would your outlook on life be different?
10. Do I love myself and my loved ones enough to attempt to live a proper life?

If you have any negative feelings about any of these questions, it's probably because you could use improvement in some or many of the aspects of living positive life these personal questions address. If so, or if not, don't sweat it. Let's just get to work regardless of anything. You're not going to achieve results by taking a pill, playing on the phone all day and night, answering questions, or running your mouth. Results won't come from a miracle machine, a wonder pill, a brand-new dietary regimen, or any other type of trick and gimmick of the health and fitness world. It's surely not going to come by sitting on our butts, is it? Not one of the aspects discussed before will do anything by itself. It must be a combination of all aspects of health, fitness, and wellness in unison. Just as we need all of the nutrients, it's not just one thing or one particular nutrient but everything available—all the elements! We've got to combine everything provided by nature, to gain the greatest health and lives.

Miracle Machines and Gizmos

Millions of dollars in advertising have been devoted to miracle machines and gizmos. Millions of wasted dollars have been spent on equipment that doesn't work or just gets boring after a few days. Why is the American public so susceptible to these miracle machines and other types of tricks/gimmicks of fitness/health? The same reason as they are in the shape that they are in, they want a shortcut to fitness/health. They're mentally lazy, probably lacking in life energy, and want the easy way out or believe they don't have the time to stay active/exercise and eat properly. I'll repeat: when dealing with the human anatomy, there are no shortcuts. It must be a lifetime commitment and we must do all the right things if we want a right result. Living nature's intended way is the only way. Anything else is tantamount to an abomination of nature. The only thing that can come out of this is a mutated species. By mutated, meaning obesity, every manner of sickness and diseases, etc.

Secondly, exercise alone is not the key to proper health. These advertisers don't tell you that without proper diet, all the exercise in the world is useless. Like we keep saying, there is a recipe for wellness and we must follow it if we are to be successful.

Why Aren't I Achieving Gains?

If I'm eating like the world is coming to an end, eating too much and nothing right, working out daily and gaining weight, and looking sloppy, a bell should go off in my head. Perhaps, if I reduce the amount and type of my diet and learn to eat quality food, maybe I'll start seeing results! The average mind can't or doesn't work that way, unless they were given the information I'm giving here. As I've said, the people in the medical industry who should be giving this knowledge have no interest. They also know little to nothing about such things, and are only trained in the pharmaceutical sciences. We've got to do a combination of varied exercises as well as varied diet to be that healthy machine we desire, but not necessarily lean (by chart standards). I truly believe that carrying more body fat than the recommended charts is not necessarily unhealthy, but excessive body fat is a death warrant and a recipe for disease.

I have had to come to the conclusion, after seeing many people who work out daily, like high aerobics and weight training, but they still maintain some fat or bulk, that genetics seems to be a determining factor in body types. Some people are big and some people are small—there are no set determining factors. If you're exercising and eating properly but don't look the way you think you should, guess what?

You are what you are. Don't get discouraged and stop exercising or doing work, because doing so is a death wish. *Everyone's not going to be a fitness model*! As we age, there will be changes that occur, but once again, the more you put into being healthy, the more you'll get out of it, and that's the God's honest truth. One thing I can say for sure is, you'll still look better than most Americans and have a stronger immune system, because most don't do a thing. The more you put into it, the more you will get out of it.

What Works

Running, walking, riding bikes, steppers, aerobics, gymnastics, Pilates, hiking, boxing, yoga, martial arts, weight training, boot camps, and CrossFit—all these things and more work. We can never stop. There are so many activities of which people can engage in. Why would they just sit and rot away? I know for a fact that when people are young, they really can't foresee life later; you always think you'll always be young. If they realized that they would turn out to be sickly, unhealthy, and prematurely old, they would not live as unhealthy of lives as they do.

It really happens before you realize. One day, you're young and vibrant, and the next day, you're fat and old. Before you know it, you're really out of shape and headed in a downward spiral, of doctors, sickness and diseases, medicine, hospitals, and doctor bills! The terrible thing about today is, many parents are starting the devastating health practices before the child is even born, and many infants today are obese or on the straight road to lives of obesity and numerous health issues because of the facts.

We've got to realize that exercise or physical activity is what the body needs, and that's movement. Stagnation and sedentary lifestyles are the big killers. Not only is exercise fun but it keeps the blood flowing, and it builds strength and stamina, which means the heart is pumping/strengthening, which means cells are more readily generating, and regenerating decreases degeneration. Degeneration of cells is what ages us and are the causes or are what allow the proliferation of the preventable diseases, and since the immune system is totally weakened, the communicable diseases too. We want to keep that process of degeneration to a minimum, so we don't look old too early and get sick and die too quickly.

Let's look at a few of the preventable diseases.

Heart Disease and/or Atherosclerosis

We will discuss here a few of the preventable diseases that so many Americans are stricken with today. They are called the preventable diseases because if you live the right way, you don't get them in the great majority of cases.

Heart disease is the #1 killer of Americans! You have the opportunity to prevent this, though, and really easily. Atherosclerosis refers to the buildup of fatty deposits in your blood vessels that could trigger heart attacks and strokes. The current scientific understanding of atherosclerosis is based upon the very simplistic notion that the cholesterol we ingest is somehow deposited on the walls of our heart and brain arteries, eventually causing obstructions, blockages, and eventually a heart attack or stroke.

The human body isn't that poorly constructed that it would just deposit excess fat on the inner linings of the very blood vessels that support life, unless it was trying to protect those vessels. The newest scientific evidence supports the notion that the fatal buildup of atherosclerosis occurs after the inner linings of arteries have become thickened and damaged. It's believed that the deposits of fatty material protects the injury and halts the damage. It's a temporary fix or Band-Aid solution from the harmful effects of modern civilization. The fatty buildup is nature's way of protecting the body from internally/externally caused degeneration of the heart and circulatory system. However, in the end, this buildup clogs the passage ways and eventually causes heart attack or some type of heart episode.

Stress, hypertension, smoking, the SAD or Standard American Diet, lack of exercise, and elevated homocysteine which a toxic amino acid, appear to be the major causes of injury to the inner linings of our blood vessels. In other words, the everyday life of the majority of Americans.

Homocysteine has a direct toxic effect on the inner lining of human blood vessels. It appears to cause coronary artery disease and strokes by injuring the lining of the arteries regardless of the level of cholesterol in the blood. Actually, the majority of people with significant coronary disease have been found to have normal cholesterol levels.

What causes homocysteine levels to build up? The most important factor causing elevated blood homocysteine levels appears to be the inadequate intake of B vitamins, including folic acid, B6, and B12, which are required to break down homocysteine in the body. Yet this is more an indication of systemic malnutrition and not just the absence of one particular nutrient or a few, but all the nutrients necessary for life. That one nutrient may be important in that function, but it shows the lack of all nutrients that are necessary for life in that person's blood. So, such a person would be susceptible to any number of the various preventable diseases because of their internal imbalances and nutritional deficiencies.

It is important to be aware of the fact that homocysteine is mostly a by-product of the body's metabolism of red meat, low-quality cheese, and other pasteurized dairy products. Other factors proven to increase homocysteine are cigarette smoking, lack of exercise, and excessive processed food and processed coffee consumption. Extensive research carried out in Holland indicated that merely the combination of smoking, coffee consumption, and lack of proper nutrient intake from right food, can increase the rate of cardiovascular disease by 40 percent. (Info from the internet.)

Proper nutritional intake, coupled with regular exercise, is of utmost importance. Quit smoking, eat a high-fiber, non-GMO diet, and limit drinking processed coffee to no more than two cups a day. Finally, limiting your red meat intake should have a significant impact on keeping your homocysteine level within a normal range; and with that highly fibrous diet, which cleanses the digestive tract and blood, our health and longevity will certainly improve. Isn't that enough reason for us to eat right, exercise, and take your vitamins and minerals, preferably from natural food or plant sources, on a daily basis?

TAKING CONTROL
OF OUR HEALTH

This is why we must learn and take control of our own health and fitness, thus, control our own destiny and lives. Don't sit back and say, "What's gonna happen is gonna happen!" You have the ability this instance to change your destiny. If not for your own sake, then for the ones that care for you and love you. Our most important commodity: our children, grandchildren, and other loved ones. What we teach them in childhood will be what they know of life. So we must teach them how from day one to live properly, so that life can be fruitful and lengthy.

In the United States especially, most of the protein in our diets comes from animal sources. Few other countries in the world depend on animal sources as much as America. Recently, researchers at the National Academy of Science's Institute of Medicine announced that "there are no known benefits and possibly some risks in eating diets with a high meat content." There is well-known, well-documented evidence of the risk involved in a meat laden diet. (info from the internet)

For the benefit of good health as well as your loves ones, lower your intake of flesh type food, especially red meat. The risk of colon cancer, breast cancer, and prostate cancer is greatly increased with a diet heavy in red meat. The good thing is that reduction or omission of red meat directly correlates to improved health. Medical research shows that people with a diet low in meats or without meats have notably lower rates of heart disease, diabetes, and gallstones. It also lowers bad cholesterol significantly, and when combined with exercise and stress reduction, can actually reverse coronary artery damage. (info from the internet.)

If you want to improve your health, lower and stabilize your weight, and feel alive with energy and vitality. Then, add more vegetables, fruits, superfood, and herbs into your diet. The healthiest diet you can eat is one based primarily on plant food, fresh vegetables, fruits, beans, and grains, as opposed to animal muscle and organs. The evidence is so convincing that the chair of the nutrition department at the Harvard School of Public Health attest that "it's no longer debatable" that "largely vegetarian diets are healthy as you can get." (Info from the internet.)

Secondly, think about it, if you burn your flesh, do you think that the protein and other substances in the flesh are unchanged? Just as your skin or organs become chemically altered, so does the skin and organs of other animals. Yes, these substances are high in protein and such, but once fire is induced, everything becomes chemically altered, and so then is destroyed. It becomes, in essence, a low-grade poison. There is much documentation as to the effects of highly cooked and overcooked meats/food, that they are drained of nutritional value. Remember, moderation is the key. If not inundated, the body has the ability to rid itself of these unusable substances as long as there is high-fiber intake and ample water.

Real-Life Reasons to Eat Less Flesh

1. Fruits and vegetables have protective properties against gastrointestinal cancer and even smoking-related cancers, including cancers of the stomach, mouth, larynx, colon, lung, esophagus, and bladder.
2. People who eat a largely vegetarian diet have lower incidents of cardiovascular disease, high blood pressure, and noninsulin-dependent diabetes compared to meat eaters.
3. A largely vegetarian diet reduces the risk of osteoporosis, kidney stones, gallstones, and many of the preventable diseases.
4. Women who eat less red meat have less breast cancer. Men who eat less red meat have less prostate cancer.

Limiting meat intake reduces amounts of saturated fats and cholesterol, but plant food itself has properties that protect the heart in other ways:

1. The sticky soluble fiber in plants such as beans, peas, oats, and barley helps to lower blood cholesterol.
2. Fruits and vegetables are excellent sources of the life-giving nutrients that can reduce the risk of heart disease.
3. The antioxidants in fruits and vegetables can help protect the heart from cholesterol damage.

So as you can see it's a win-win situation when we engage in a diet of natural life-energy plant food. We have got to learn to adjust our taste buds toward these life-giving and lifesaving food. Let's forget about McDonald's, pizza, and processed and refined food, and start eating the food of our own existence. Man doesn't come out of a test tube (yet!), and neither should our diets consist of nonlife-giving materials. (Info from the internet.)

Diabetes

1. If you are overweight or obese, it is more likely that you have type 2 diabetes.
2. If you suddenly developed signs of diabetes, such as frequent urination, unusual thirst and hunger, and weight loss, perhaps after an illness, and are a young adult or child, it is more likely that you have type 1 diabetes. However, in these more modern times, it could very well be type 2.
3. If you are not overweight and there are ketones in your urine, it is more likely that you have type 1 diabetes.
4. If you are African American or Hispanic American, are older than forty, are overweight, and haven't been feeling quite "right" for a long time, it is more likely that you have type 2 diabetes.
5. If your doctor treats you with insulin injections, you could have either type 1 or type 2 diabetes.

The risk factors associated with type 1 or type 2 diabetes are different. For both type 1 and type 2 diabetes, having a family history of diabetes puts you at a higher risk for developing the disease than for a person with no family history of diabetes. However, many people with type 1 diabetes have no known family history of the disease. Type 1 diabetes is more common among whites than among members of other racial groups. In contrast, members of Native American, African American, and Hispanic ethnic groups are at a higher risk for developing type 2 diabetes. Perhaps the genetic makeup of nonwhites predisposes them to the obesity and diabetes that tend to result from a twentieth-century sedentary American lifestyle. This is more medical information from the internet. I, however, do not necessarily concur with what they are saying, but I have added these things for information purposes only, not for what I actually believe is the case. I believe, regardless of genetics, when we live according to the rules of nature, we will attain the greatest health and lives regardless of pigmentation of skin.

A major difference in the characteristics of individuals with type 1 and type 2 diabetes is the age it begins. Typically, type 1 diabetes mainly develops in individuals under the age of forty. Half of all people diagnosed with type 1 diabetes are under the age of twenty. In contrast, most people diagnosed with type 2 diabetes are over the age of thirty, although type 2 diabetes is on the rise among teenagers and young adults. The risk of type 2 increases with age. Half of all new cases of type 2 diabetes are people aged fifty-five and older.

Type 2 diabetes is more common in overweight and obese individuals, whereas body weight does not seem to be a risk factor for type 1 diabetes. Type 2 diabetes is often found in women with a history of giving birth to babies weighing more than nine pounds and in women who were previously diagnosed with gestational diabetes. In both men and women, high blood pressure and very high concentrations of fats in the blood are more common in people with type 2 diabetes.

You can't get diabetes, either type 1 or type 2, from stress, exposure to someone who already has diabetes, or from something you ate. Although diabetes may reveal itself after an illness or a stressful experience, these may have only speeded up the appearance of the disease.

The medical industry states that there is no cure for diabetes, but it is clearly indicated through studies that a diet low in fat and sugar and rich in life-giving food (fruits and vegetables) is most beneficial to those suffering this disease of malnutrition. Along with a consistent exercise program, diabetes and the problems associated with it can be greatly curbed and or alleviated. (Info from the internet.)

Some Natural Substances from Our Own Earth

As we have said earlier, the earth has a cornucopia of medicine in their natural form throughout the earth. Many of these substances have been used and are used by man for thousands of years. These substances work in unison with the body's natural homeostatic (balancing) systems to rid the body of the disease and imbalance. There are far too many substances to even begin to list in this short book; however, I will list a few of the substances I have tried with great results. Before I began getting in to total health, I thought that those who spoke of natural healing needed psychological help. How foolish we are when we don't know; you can't know what you don't know. As I began to educate myself on these substances and to utilize them, I could not fathom why the medical industry does not advocate the use of these substances from nature before first prescribing chemical meds. Surely, the highly intelligent scientists must realize that they cannot outdo nature! Profits seem to determine their mentalities.

Products from the beehive:

1. Bee pollen
2. Honey
3. Bee propolis
4. Royal jelly

Wow! Any person that took my advice and tried one of these products came back to me with high praises, especially those who had lifetime allergies or just plain, poor-quality health

Bee Pollen

It is flower pollen collected by honeybees from a variety of plants and is the insects' primary food source. Pollen grains, which are the flowers' male reproductive cells, contain concentrations of phytochemicals and nutrients. Bee pollen is rich in carotenoids, flavonoids, and phytosterols. The exact ingredient varies depending on the plant sources, location, and growing conditions. However, beta-carotene, beta-sitosterol, isorhamnetin, kaempferol, lycopene, quercetin, and rutin are consistently reported.

Studies show promising results regarding pollen's healing potential. Pollen extract was an effective treatment for prostate enlargement and prostatitis. In another study, mice with lung cancer survived almost twice as long when treated with pollen extracts compared with untreated controls. Pollen increased the effectiveness of chemotherapy when used in unison. Unlike chemotherapy, pollen didn't attack tumors but stimulated immunity. So, in other words, pollen promotes healing naturally by strengthening immune function. (Info from the internet.)

Honey

Is a by-product of bees concentrating plant nectars into a nutritious substance. No bacteria can grow where honey is present, and honey *never* spoils. In fact, archaeologists have found honey in the ancient crypts of mummies that was still viable and edible. It is mainly food for bees, bears, and humans. The characteristic flowery taste of raw honey comes from the pollen it contains. Honey's ability to heal wounds and treat infections has been known for thousands of years. It also is known for its antioxidant, antibiotic, and antiviral capabilities, as well as cosmetic uses.

Four mechanisms are proposed for honey's healing properties:

1. Honey is mostly glucose and fructose. These sugars are strongly attracted to water, forming a viscous syrup. When spread on a wound, honey absorbs water and body fluids, thus desiccating bacteria and fungi and inhibiting their growth.
2. Raw honey contains glucose oxidase, an enzyme that, in the presence of a little water, produces hydrogen peroxide, a mild antiseptic. Glucose oxidase is destroyed by bright light, heat, and pasteurization, so it is absent from most commercial honeys.
3. Raw honey contains bee pollen, enzymes, and propolis, all of which can stimulate new tissue growth.
4. Honey can contain additional medicinal compounds, including essential oils, flavonoids, terpenes, and polyphenols, depending on the plant from which the pollen was taken. (Info from the internet.)

Propolis

Consists mainly of specific tree resins collected by honeybees. Bees use propolis like putty to seal cracks and openings in the hive, strengthen the comb, and seal brood cells. Propolis also helps with the sterilization of the hive—the resins protect both trees and bees from infections.

More than 180 compounds have been identified in propolis and many are biologically active. Flavonoids are abundant, including apigenin, galangin, kaempferol, luteolin, pinocembrin, pinostrobin, and quercetin, all of which are anti-inflammatory, spasmolytic, antiallergenic, antioxidant, and/or antimutagenic. Propolis is uniquely rich in the caffeic acid phenethyl ester, which in animal studies has inhibited cancer growth and reduced inflammation as effectively as drugs.

Propolis also contains organic acids and their derivatives as well as terpenoids. These constituents contribute antibiotic, antifungal, and antiviral effects. So, as you can see, propolis is a powerhouse, which has healing ramifications for every manner of internal negativity. (Info from the internet.)

Royal Jelly

Is a thick, creamy fluid synthesized in nurse bees' bodies during digestion of bee pollen and secreted from glands in their heads. I have personally eaten royal jelly and all the parts of the bee hive in the maintenance of my health with only the greatest results. The collection of royal jelly is a labor-intensive process that involves gently vacuuming the royal jelly from hive cells, where it is stored, and straining out the larva. All larvae are fed royal jelly for three days, but the queen bee eats royal jelly exclusively, which makes her fertile and able to live for five to seven years. In contrast, worker bees are sterile and live just seven to eight weeks. Royal jelly has a reputation for maintaining youthfulness in humans, but research, while encouraging, lags behind that for other hive products.

Fresh royal jelly is mostly totally absorbable protein. Polyunsaturated (essential) fatty acids are mainly metabolized to hydroxy fatty acids in the skin, another key ingredient of royal jelly. Hydroxy fatty acids protect skin from dehydration, and some are strongly anti-inflammatory. HFA may also be anti-inflammatory. Royal jelly also contains collagen, lecithin, and vitamins A, C, D, and E—all of which benefit the skin. Concentrated royal jelly moisturizes dry skin and soothes dermatitis. I personally have had atopic dermatitis all my life, and when I started taking bee products, I have seen this condition virtually disappear!

Additionally, royal jelly contains all the B vitamins and is especially rich in pantothenic acid. It contains phytosterols (mainly beta-sitosterol) and enzymes, as well as acetylcholine and hormones, including estradiol and testosterone. All of the compounds help lower cholesterol. (Info from the internet.)

This is just one small example of the chemical substances contained in substances from the planet earth that are beneficial to human life. It is of the utmost importance for us to learn as much as possible about as many substances provided by the earth as we possibly can. Herbs, whole food vitamins, and the naturally occurring substances from all the cultures of the world need to be learned, utilized, and made a part of a balanced life. Go to your nearest bookstore; there are numerous reference materials on natural health. Find the one that interests you the most, and teach others in your life, family, and friends. Passing on the secrets of maximum life—could there be any greater gift?

Commercial Vitamins/ Synthetic Vitamins are of No Value to Health

Millions of Americans are taking vitamins in a preventive manner in hopes of expanding good health. There are numerous vitamin supplements from numerous companies, all promoting their products as beneficial to health. The commercially promoted vitamins in general are synthetically/chemically derived products. As such, these products are of absolutely no value to cellular generation, or of little value to life and internal balance. When our body derives vitamins, they must be derived from those substances which come from nature, most times from plant but not only, as we have discussed earlier. Nature is what our bodies come from, and the nutrients provided by nature are those which the cells recognize. They have the necessary genetic markers that let the body know that these are necessary nutrients of life. Substances not of nature (inorganic) are not recognized, so they are of no benefit to health/life. The cells can't use them.

Furthermore, vitamins are of no value without necessary minerals present. Minerals are the most essential of the building blocks for our lives, and the catalyst for the absorption of vitamins by the cells. So, no matter how good the vitamins are, without minerals, they are of no value. For years, I have recommended the usage of whole food vitamin supplements, yet without the necessary minerals present, as we have said, the vitamins have little or no effect. This can be seen in the health of so many in American society. Although many people take so-called nutritional substances in a preventive manner, multitudes of people are still contracting the preventable diseases. When the necessary nutrients, or more specifically the minerals were actually present, these conditions would never manifest.

Sea nutrients are the most valuable to our lives

Did you know that nutrients from the sea contain four hundred times the nutritional value of land-based food? Learn here about the greatest food source on earth that few humans even know about.

Marine Phytoplankton

Marine phytoplankton is nutrient-dense whole food. More powerful than any other food source we have on earth, making it the most nutrient-dense whole food on the planet. All of the necessary vitamins, minerals, and nutrients can be found in it and are almost totally bioavailable to our cells, unlike land-based nutrients. It is impossible for humans/animals to derive the necessary vitamins and nutrients from the present food to promote optimum health, because the soils have become so nutrient depleted. Just a little something to consider.

There are two reasons why our soils have become so depleted, and the nutritional value and edible quality of our food have gotten so low. One is that today's agriculture does not allow for regeneration of the soil. We rely on chemical fertilizers to only replace three or four of the eight-five or so necessary minerals. Phosphorous, potassium, and nitrogen are the main ingredients in our fertilizers.

The other reason why our food are less nutritious, and less tasty too, than fifty years ago is that fruits and vegetables are picked while they are still green and haven't had the chance to extract all of the nutrients from the soil. They are harvested green, so they ripen on the way to market. Many times fruits and vegetables have to travel thousands of miles from farm to factory and finally to the store. They are harvested while still green to enable them to last longer in storage, but it also leaves insufficient time for the plant to fully absorb whatever minerals are available in the soil and to synthesize vitamins and other nutrients. The ripening process continues, cut off from the soil and sun, in doing so, we render those food, minimally nutritious and of the lowest edible quality.

Supplementation Is Paramount

This is why we must learn about the numerous, varied natural nutrients from the land and the sea. In this way, we maximize our health/lives with the abundance of life-giving energy. Without the necessary energy of life, we hasten our cells' electrical potential to zero. Once our cell energy hits zero, it's lights out! Life-giving products put life into the cells of our body, promoting and maximizing life. It's your responsibility to learn as much as is humanly possible about the abundance of life that nature has provided for all life to thrive.

Shilajit

Summary of Scientific Studies of *Shilajit*

Over sixty years of clinical research have shown that fulvic acid, or humic acid, also known as the humates, and in India it's called *shilajit*, is a nutritional powerhouse. For purposes here, we will just use shilajit and not the many other names.

Shilajit has positive effects on humans. It increases longevity, improves memory and cognitive ability, reduces allergies and respiratory problems, reduces stress, and relieves digestive troubles. It is anti-inflammatory, antioxidant, and eliminates free radicals. The research proves that *shilajit* increases immunity, strength, and endurance, and lives up to its ancient reputation as the "destroyer of weakness."

Technically, *shilajit* is an exudate that is pressed out from layers of rock in the most sacred and highest mountains in Nepal and other areas. It is composed of humus and organic plant material that has been compressed by layers of rock. Humus is formed when soil microorganisms decompose animal and plant material into elements usable by plants. Plants are the source of all our food, and humus is the source of plant food. Unlike other soil humus, *shilajit* humus consists of 60–80 percent organic mass.

About two hundred million years ago, India was a large island off the Australian coast separated from the Eurasian continent by the Tethys Sea. The Indian continent drifted north at a rate of about nine meters a century. This movement led to the eventual disappearance of the Tethys Sea. Fifty million years ago, the Indian continent collided with the Asian continent. This caused the seabed of the Tethys Sea to be pushed up and keep moving up to eventually form the Himalayan mountains. The Himalayan mountains continue to rise more than one centimeter a year. During this transition, the mineral-rich and fertile soil of the seabed gave rise to a lush and dense tropical jungle. As the ground continued to be pushed up to become mountains, a lot of the plants became trapped by layers of rock and soil and remained preserved for thousands of years. These plants had never been exposed to any chemicals, fertilizers, or pesticides. They are gradually transformed into humus, a rich organic mass that is food for new plant life.

What are humic substances? They are the end result of all once-living organisms, mostly plants, disassembled by nature's natural decomposition and recycling processes, then highly refined by millions of species of beneficial soil-based microorganisms. Finally processed by microscopic plants, such as yeast, algae, mold, fungi, etc., that finish up the process. These tiny beneficial plants refine, purify, combine, and re-refine, until tons of once-living matter are converted to pounds and ounces. Yet like a miracle, when it is all said and done, the end product is not inert basic "dead" mineral elements but is transformed into the world's most complex and ultracompact molecules. Even the nucleic acids, RNA and DNA, of the earlier life-forms remain intact. The molecules are ultracondensed and highly functional, rolled up into tight little balls that are supercharged biochemical and phytochemical power plants, similar to storage batteries or fuel cells. Where did this supercharged power come from? It is sunshine light energy captured during plant photosynthesis, and through decomposition, it is converted and stored within the interior of the world's most refined and complex molecules.

Humic substances are considered nature's own best medicine for plants, animals, humans, and the earth itself. This lowly soil substance has the ability to clean up the earth's environment, neutralize radiation and deadly toxins, heal the agricultural lands, fuel the spark of life in living organisms, disarm and kill infectious pathogens, destroy the deadliest viruses, prevent most, if not all diseases, and even cure and restore diseased and damaged tissues and organs in plants, animals, and man.

Buckminster Fuller, one of America's best known thinkers of the twentieth century, helps us to understand how plants accumulate energy from the photosynthesis of the sun. Visualize a log burning in the fireplace. When asked "what is fire," Buckminster explained, in a long tirade, that fire is the sun's radiation unwinding. Each growth ring of the tree's log represents a year. He explained that many years of the sun's flame winding through the sky, absorbed by the tree through photosynthesis, is now unwinding in the burning log. With a log of firewood, lump of coal, oil, natural gas, or gasoline, all of which are the remains of once-living plants, it is easy to see and understand solar energy storage and release. With the humic substances, it is not so clear to see because they don't readily burn but are powerpacked with the energy of millions of years.

Humic substances are found in rich humus soil in trace amounts. They are also found in massive ancient plant deposits, never truly fossilized, still remaining completely organic. What makes their stored solar energy so different? The key is found in nature's decomposition and refining process. The energy is converted into a different form. Coal, oil, tar, natural gas, and uranium deposits all are "dead," inorganic remnants of ancient plants. Uranium mines, just like coal mines and tar pits, also have fossilized trees, leaves, and dinosaur bones, all remnants of ancient life turned to rock.

Uranium ore is rock and doesn't burn, or does it? Ponder how a few pounds of seemingly inert refined uranium ore has the power to fuel the reactor in a nuclear power plant or become an atomic bomb. Where is all of that energy stored? The power is deep within complex molecules and is released through nuclear fission, the splitting of the atom's nucleus. Is that similar to the seemingly inert humic substances? Humic substances are not radioactive, but they can quickly and effectively neutralize radiation.

87

To sum it all up, humic substances consist of a fantastic array of powerful phytochemicals, biochemicals, supercharged antioxidants, free-radical scavengers, superoxide dismutase, nutrients, enzymes, hormones, amino acids, antibiotics, antivirals, antifungals, etc. Many of the substances that make up humic matter have yet to be discovered and cataloged among the known and documented organic chemicals.

So as we can see, the awesome power of nature, just in these few substances from the earth of prehistoric origin and current-day origin, are the catalysts and energizers for all living matter. This means they are something highly beneficial to our lives. We must continue to educate ourselves about the numerous substances provided for our lives by nature. When we have such knowledge, we have little to no need ever for chemical poisons, but if we do, our bodies are so strengthened that the chemical poisons can work and then our strong, properly nourished bodies can bring themselves back into balance. When we put chemical poisons in an already decimated body, with little to no immune function, those chemical poisons cause more problems than the diseases themselves.

Children's Wellness and Fitness

Of equal or more importance to our health than our own is the health of our children! I say more, because an adult has the right to make their own decisions in life. It is our responsibility to bring our children up in such a way that they will understand the benefits of healthy living. We must teach them from an early age about what food is good for them and which ones are not. You are not being kind to your child just because you allow them to eat and thus enjoy junk or bad food, which are poison to the body and only cause disease and death. You are actually doing them an injustice, that eventually will cause only misery and suffering. Why should we not give our children the best that life has to offer? Mother Nature has provided more than enough bounty for you to never have to go to McDonald's or some other disease-peddling, so-called food chain.

The first thing we must do if we are not healthy is to learn ourselves what is healthy and beneficial and what is not. Although there are many food for you to choose, it is really up to you to investigate and realize that much of the food in America are compromised. We still must do what we have to do to make the best lives possible.

The first years of life are when the main learning phases of life are enacted. We learn language, we learn how to walk, to talk, and we learn the type of food that we are fed. You must begin from the first years to feed your child food that is healthy as well as tasty. The natural food is the only one that is acceptable.

My children, who are now adults, were brought up on healthy but very tasty food. Fruits, vegetables, minimal meats, sea life, all the normal things. The only difference was that the food was exclusively from mostly natural sources. Meaning, hardly any canned, frozen, or processed food as their mother wouldn't allow it. Their mother, who is now deceased, was from Costa Rica. I have observed that people from the Caribbean and Central and South Americas have a much better and more diverse diet than their American counterparts. That can also be said of numerous other people in various parts of the world. My four-year-old that is living in the Philippines is being raised in the same natural ways, and of course, she stays active.

Mainly only in America are processed, frozen, synthesized, microwaved, grease-filled, unnatural food promoted as real food. No wonder more than two-thirds of Americans are overweight. No wonder that our hospitals and health systems are overwhelmed with a generally sick population. No wonder hospital and insurance costs are astronomical. The bad part is it doesn't have to be that way. Just eat right, sleep right, exercise, and guess what, strong immune systems, strong respiratory systems, strong muscles and bones, cosmetic beauty, making for a well-rounded and positive individual. Overweight people and those who have health issues almost always have self-esteem problems, which lead to depression, which is a precursor or promoter of disease. Finding high-quality food, however, is problematic for many Americans since American food is of the lowest quality, but do the best you can and are financially able to.

Life Starts from the First Day

Let's start from day one. Mother's milk versus chemical, man-made formula. The prevailing thoughts are that babies require mothers' milk for optimal health, since that is why nature provided it—for the sustenance of infant humans. The baby formula industry, which makes billions of dollars a year, would like nothing more than for you to bring your baby up on their poison formulas. That's job security for the medical/pharmaceutical businesses who probably own them. They say it's safe, convenient, scientific; it's the best. It goes back to what I have been preaching—man has yet to circumvent nature. I don't think it's possible. As a matter of fact, I know it's impossible for man to be a greater asset to nature and mankind than nature itself.

The truth is that the benefits of breastfeeding go far beyond scientific measurements and what most may know. We do know that breast milk passes the mother's antibodies to her infant. This protects the baby during infancy and beyond from a host of diseases that infants are susceptible to. What they cannot measure is the psychological and physical bonds that happen between mother and baby during the feeding process. I doubt if that can ever be measured and known.

Breast milk is far easier to digest than formula; therefore, babies are less likely to experience gastrointestinal problems. Bottle-fed babies do sleep longer because formula is slow to digest. There is medical evidence to prove that breastfed babies grow up to have lower cholesterol levels and lower rates of heart disease as adults. Iron deficiency is less frequent in breastfed babies. Certain enzymes in breast milk have the power to lower the incidence of allergies, diarrhea, upper respiratory infections, otitis media, sinusitis, pneumonia, blood poisoning, meningitis, botulism, urinary tract infections, enterocolitis, and sudden death syndrome in both infants and children. (Info from the internet.)

Breastfed babies become ill nearly half as frequently as bottle-fed babies. Recent surveys indicate that breastfed babies are less prone to becoming overweight adults. There is also strong evidence that breastfeeding decreases the incidence of diabetes, Crohn's disease, ulcerative colitis, and lymphoma during adulthood. (Info from the internet.)

Formula is full of chemicals, synthesized vitamins, fats (saturated), glycerides, refined salt, refined sugar, none of which contain life energy and all of them compromise health while disrupting systems. I cannot say, however, that bottle-feeding is wrong. Some women are unable to breastfeed, but that does not make you a bad person. If you can, however, the benefits to yourself and your child make it worth the time. If you can't, then this is the time when you should begin to feed your child from another mother who can nourish your child: Mother Nature. Find what natural milk and food will be of the most benefit to your child, not formula! (Info from the internet.)

Each stage of the human life cycle benefits from the life energy in breast milk. Breastfeeding definitely protects the mother by reducing her blood loss after birth and by improving her bone mineralization, so that risk of hip fractures during menopause decreases. It also appears that the mother's risk of ovarian and breast cancer is less when they breastfeed. (Info from the internet.)

As your children progress, your children will eat what you eat. That's where they form their eating habits as well as all other things they know in life. They learn from you! You can teach them from the earliest stages what are the good food and what are the bad ones, and don't give them to them. Don't worry as they'll listen and follow your advice; they're not teenagers yet. This is the time when you can show them the food with life energy: the fruits and vegetables and all their vibrant colors. So many things can be learned just from teaching them about fruits, vegetables, and other plant food. Counting, colors, and just general nutrition, all will only add to their knowledge of life and living right. Don't depend on the school system to educate them about healthy living. From last I heard, they're still serving green hot dogs for lunch and peddling chocolate for fund-raisers. If your child is normal (no birth defects) and is fat, unhealthy, and out of shape, then whose fault do you think it is, the child's? It is our responsibility to educate them on what's right and wrong, and to ensure that they are healthy and fit. It is our responsibility to raise them in the healthiest manners possible.

Everyone talks about the need for five servings of fruit and five servings of vegetables a day. Not many people are doing that; it's just not realistic. We can, however, not buy junk food or the numerous pseudo food they have in the market today. We must continually reinforce how good and tasty fresh fruit and vegetables are to our young. Keep lots of oranges, bananas, grapes, kiwi, strawberries, carrots, tomatoes, potatoes (not french fries), and lettuce around. Unfortunately, the people must wake up and fight against these unhealthy GMOs, but for now they are all that are available in most cases. They really are a scourge to nature and mankind. They are one of the roots of the problems with the dying of the honeybees who pollinate the food of the earth. A child will eventually learn to eat what is there. Supplementation of necessary nutrients can be found in naturally based minerals, vitamins, herbs, and naturally based synergistic mixtures. Stay away from highly commercial, synthetic, or chemically based concoctions as they contain none of the life-giving material needed for cellular production and growth. They are just more junk!

I suggest the blending of food with high-powered blenders like the Vitamix company has available. It is one of the best ways to get the necessary amounts of nutrients, and without actually having to chew all that food. Furthermore, the food is already broken down for easier assimilation to the cells. Juicing is also very beneficial, but with juicing, we lose 65 percent of the nutrients which are present in the fiber, seeds, stems, skin, etc.

Fish and poultry can be introduced after the first year. Unless organic, wild, and or high-quality red meat is just not good or necessary. Keep it to a minimum or preferably eliminate it. Remember, concentrate on teaching your children about food that contain life energy, because this is necessary knowledge on their long road to long, enjoyable, positive life, hopefully a disease-free life. Also, "We are what we eat." So if you eat crappy food . . .

And just as we must do for ourselves, we must create an environment that is conducive to positive life in all aspects. We must have a positive outlook, and in turn your child will also have these positive outlooks. In saying so, we must also not allow our children to dictate to us; we are the parents. We must not allow too much time sitting around playing video games and doing nothing constructive. There are so many things to do that are not sedentary in nature, but we've got to have the motivation, and so do they. We are their motivation. Our motivation is our knowledge that unhealthy eating and sedentary lifestyle is an invitation to heartache and disease. Loving parents would not want their children to suffer for so ludicrous a reason as being unhealthy now, would we?

Just because you don't believe you have health problems now, doesn't mean that they are not forthcoming. For most in America these days, sickness and disease begin to manifest in childhood. If you are living like the typical American, then you are eating a diet that consists of 90 percent cooked, processed, packaged, adulterated, even irradiated, and definitely genetically-engineered food. They are filled with chemicals and preservatives, grown in nutrient depleted soil, and stored on shelves for long periods of time, resulting in massive nutritional loss. All this adds up to is a "dead food diet." The body cannot build strong new cells and maintain a healthy immune system to prevent disease when it's receiving lifeless food. Continuation of misguided eating habits and just plain poor eating habits will prevent the body from functioning normally as nature intended. Dead food are dead, soon to decay matter, they don't promote or encourage life, and a body without life-giving nourishment is as good as dead! "The fountain of youth cannot exist under these circumstances."

Malnutrition is already manifesting itself in our children; obesity and high blood cholesterol, heart disease, type 2 diabetes, and cancers of all types are examples. The young may turn to drugs because of depression resulting from their poor diets, lack of self-esteem, and just poor health, looking for a way to feel good. Many children never eat raw fruits or vegetables, but subsist on a diet high in fat, sugar, and salt. We even see children with sodas in their hands at breakfast time, if they even get a breakfast. The right food can and do heal, just as the wrong food can cause sickness, rapid aging, and in time, premature death! Children are having heart attacks and are contracting type 2 diabetes at unprecedented rates. It's a crime to feed and thus destine your child to die from food that can cause disease, when all you have to do is feed them the food that were provided for our lives, not what man creates! The numerous addictions and health problems are manifested and find their root in unhealthy living.

Everybody in the American community seems to be sick on drugs (legal and illegal), smoke cigarettes, eat the worst food, and are happy with being fat and out of shape! This makes absolutely no sense! Let's start living like human beings are supposed to, and stop eating/drinking and doing things that can only sicken, and kill us while enriching the few!

We could talk on to infinity, but that is not what people who need to get healthy need to do. Action, in this instance, very much so, speaks louder than words. I can tell you till I'm blue in the face that eating right, exercising, expanding your knowledge of natural healing, sleeping right, and maintaining a positive attitude are what will give you the keys to health. But until you actually implement these things yourself, all they will be is words. As I have said earlier, if not for your sake, then for the sake of your children. It is our responsibility to ensure that they are given the greatest opportunity at long, useable, healthy, successful, positive, loving life! #Stayyoungnaturally #Recipeforwellness

Namaste

TESLA
Holistic / Preventive Wellness

WWW.TESLALONGLIFE.COM

NATURAL HEALING & WELLNESS COACHING

If you're looking for preventive health advice from dependable and experienced practitioners then, TESLA Wellness offers wellness coaching for people living in the modern age. Here, we share the many secrets of natural health/wellness with you the client about making healthy living choices, to include living an active lifestyle, which allows you to realize and attain your best health. As your wellness coaching team, we'll guide you along the way and help you find the most effective and efficient ways to build optimum health. Our founder, Darius Wright, had to suffer the effects of an unhealthy lifestyle for decades before he finally got tired of being sick and tired! Although he was always a high level athlete in multiple sports, his life took him to the brink of death, on several occasions throughout his first 3 and a half decades of life. From that life of living death, he took it upon himself to learn the truth about health and wellness. Today, he uses TESLA Wellness to share this knowledge gained from great suffering, and great research, with those wishing to attain the greatest possible health for themselves and families. For those looking to create positive changes in their lives, we welcome you to utilize our wellness consultation services. Set up a consultation with one of our practitioners and get REAL life counseling for your specific health/wellness needs by contacting us today.

About Us

TESLA Wellness offers the latest in natural health and wellness coaching for those looking to improve their health. Utilizing the simplistic natural methods and tools given to us by the Earth and the knowledge gained through our evolution. We help create better humans through information, counseling, and a range of products that offer a variety of benefits to all of our clients. In other words, we help you attain the knowledge, the pride, and the commitment to make optimum health and wellness, a reality.

Our founder, Darius Wright, began his path as an athlete, and just regular person who believed in all the same things that everyone else did, in reference to health/wellness. Over the years of working with people in the fitness world and a lifetime of improperly living/eating, the devolving to a life of addictions, mental depressions, and just a totally negative life, that without change, would have ended many years ago. He decided to make a change for the better, or death would be the only result. Now, after more than 25 years of experience as a holistic practitioner, and natural healer, he shares what he's learned through TESLA Wellness. We all have the same abilities to thrive in this life, but we must first attain the knowledge. Contact us today to learn more about living a healthier, more fruitful life! Always remember, we must all learn to, Stay young and healthy naturally! It'll only make you better!